The Economics of Cryptocu

C000126816

Cryptocurrencies have had a profound effect on financial markets worldwide. This edited book aims to explore the economic implications of the use of cryptocurrencies. Drawing from chapter contributors from around the world, the book will be a valuable resource on the economics of cryptocurrencies. The intended audience is composed of academics, corporate leaders, entrepreneurs, government leaders, consultants and policy makers worldwide.

Over the past few years, the topic of cryptocurrencies has gained global attention and has been the subject of discussion in various news media, in policy-making bodies and government entities, and in financial institutions, classrooms and boardrooms. Despite widespread interest, much remains unknown on what the economic implications of cryptocurrencies are. This book enhances the reader's understanding of cryptocurrencies, its impact on industry and its implications on the political and economic environment. Drawing from chapter contributions from leading academics and thought leaders from around the world, this book is the definitive guide on the economics of cryptocurrencies.

There is scarcity of well conceived, academically grounded literature on the impact of cryptocurrencies on industry, politics and economics. This pioneering book provides up-to-date and in-depth analysis on the subject. The book will be appealing to academic communities, business professionals and entrepreneurs in their quest for better understanding the challenges and opportunities brought about by cryptocurrencies. Consultants, government officials and policy makers will find the information helpful in defining strategic pathways into the future.

J. Mark Munoz is Professor of Management at Millikin University and former Visiting Fellow at the Kennedy School of Government at Harvard University. He is a recipient of several awards including four Best Research Paper Awards, two international book awards, a literary award and the ACBSP Teaching Excellence Award, among others. Aside from top-tier journal publications, he has authored/edited/coedited more than 20 books in management and economics such as *Handbook on the Geopolitics of Business*, *Advances in Geoeconomics* and *Global Business Intelligence*. As Chairman/CEO of the international management consulting firm Munoz and Associates International, he directs and manages consulting projects for companies worldwide.

Michael Frenkel is Professor of Macroeconomics and International Economics at WHU–Oitto Beisheim School of Management. He is also the Director of the Center for European Studies (CEUS) at WHU. He received his diploma degree in economics and his doctoral degree from the University of Mainz, Germany. He has extensive international experience resulting from his work with the International Monetary Fund and from various visiting positions, among them with the Harvard University Summer School, the University of Michigan, Georgetown University, Carnegie Mellon University, Emory University, Brandeis University and Chulalongkorn University (Thailand). He serves on the editorial board of the *Global Finance Journal*, the *Journal of Economics and Statistics* and the *Journal for Markets and Ethics*.

Routledge International Studies in Money and Banking

The Economics of Cryptocurrencies

Edited by J. Mark Munoz
and Michael Frenkel

Routledge
Taylor & Francis Group

LONDON AND NEW YORK

First published 2021
by Routledge
2 Park Square, Milton Park, Abingdon, Oxon OX14 4RN

and by Routledge
52 Vanderbilt Avenue, New York, NY 10017

Routledge is an imprint of the Taylor & Francis Group, an informa business

British Library Cataloguing-in-Publication Data
A catalogue record for this book is available from the British Library

Library of Congress Cataloging-in-Publication Data
Names: Munoz, J. Mark, editor. | Frenkel, Michael, 1954– editor.
Title: The economics of cryptocurrencies / edited by J. Mark Munoz and
    Michael Frenkel.
Description: 1 Edition. | New York : Routledge, 2020. | Series:
    Routledge international studies in money and banking | Includes
    bibliographical references and index.
Identifiers: LCCN 2020030099 (print) | LCCN 2020030100 (ebook) |
    ISBN 9780367191030 (hardback) | ISBN 9780429200427 (ebook)
Subjects: LCSH: Cryptocurrencies. | Technological innovations—
    Economic aspects.
Classification: LCC HG1710 .E176 2020 (print) | LCC HG1710 (ebook) |
    DDC 332.4—dc23
LC record available at https://lccn.loc.gov/2020030099
LC ebook record available at https://lccn.loc.gov/2020030100

ISBN: 978-0-367-19103-0 (hbk)
ISBN: 978-0-429-20042-7 (ebk)

Typeset in Bembo
by Apex CoVantage, LLC

Contents

Illustrations

Figures

Tables

Contributors

Jean-Marie Ayer is Professor of Innovation and Entrepreneurship at the HEG School of Management Switzerland and director of the research program on the application of blockchain technologies at the University of Applied Sciences of Western Switzerland (HES-SO). He has more than 25 years of executive experience in large corporations and is the founder of several start-ups.

Cristiano Bellavitis is Lecturer (Assistant Professor) of Innovation and Entrepreneurship at the Faculty of Management and International Business of Auckland Business School. Cristiano obtained his doctorate in management from Cass Business School, London. His research interests include network theory, strategic partnering and interfirm networking in entrepreneurial finance settings, and creative industries. His work has been published in leading international journals such as the *British Journal of Management, Journal of Small Business Management, Managerial and Decision Economics, Venture Capital* and *Journal of General Management*.

Silvia Dal Bianco is a teaching fellow at UCL–Economics. Her areas of expertise include applied and international economics as well as macroeconomics. Her current research focuses on cryptocurrencies, technological change and financial crises. Before joining academia, Silvia has consulted a number of national and international institutions, such as UNESCO, DFID and the Italian Ministry of Foreign Trade.

Suleika Bort is Full Professor and head of the Chair of Organization and International Management at the Faculty of Economics and Business Administration at Chemnitz University of Technology, Germany. Previously she worked as Lecturer in International Business at the University of Sydney and as post-doc at the chair of SME Research and Entrepreneurship at Mannheim University, Germany. She also received her PhD thesis in Organizational Behavior from Mannheim University. Suleika has published in leading management outlets such as *Journal of Management Studies, Organization Studies, Journal of International Business Studies* and *Academy of Management Proceedings* and has received a number of awards.

Carlos M. DaSilva is Professor of Entrepreneurship at the HEG School of Management Switzerland, runs the Founder Institute Start-up Accelerator Program in Lisbon and is a lead trainer at the National Swiss Innovation Agency (INNOSUISSE) for early stage financing. His research has been published in peer-reviewed academic journals such as *Long Range Planning*, and he is the author of the book *Entrepreneurial Finance: A Global Perspective.*

Allison Derrick is a research economist in the International Directorate of the Bureau of Economic Analysis. Her current projects include the economic measurements of new technologies, trade in IT services and intellectual property transfers within multinational enterprises. She holds a PhD in Agricultural and Applied Economics from the University of Wisconsin–Madison, where she specialized in international trade and economic development.

Michael Frenkel is a tenured Full Professor of Macroeconomics and International Economics and Associate Dean at WHU–Otto Beisheim School of Management, Germany. He got his diploma degree in economics and his doctoral degree from the University of Mainz, Germany. His extensive international experience stems from working for several years with the International Monetary Fund and from visiting positions with Harvard University Summer School, the University of Michigan Business School, Georgetown University, Carnegie Mellon University, Emory University, Brandeis University and several other international universities. He has more than 100 publications in the fields of macroeconomics and international finance. He is the coauthor of two standard German textbooks covering growth theory and national income accounting and contributed to several books. He serves on the editorial board of the *Global Finance Journal*, the *Journal of Economics and Statistics* and the *Journal for Markets and Ethics.*

Björn Holste is Managing Partner at Technology Institute. He holds a master's degree in Mechanical Engineering and Business Administration, as well as a doctoral degree in macroeconomics from the University of Kaiserslautern. He has 20 years of professional experience in the financial industry with a focus on quantitative asset management with major financial institutions like UBS and Deutsche Bank on the managing director level. Björn serves as lecturer for several German universities and has an extensive background in major programming languages.

Andrew Isaak, MBA, is Assistant Professor at Solbridge International School of Business in South Korea. His doctoral dissertation at the University of Mannheim, Germany, empirically explores crowdfunding and cryptocurrencies from a management science perspective with a focus on cross-national studies. He has published a book with Wiley and book chapters with Edward Elgar and has received Best Reviewer Awards from the 2018 Academy of Management (AOM) Conference and from Junior Management Science (JMS).

Valtteri Kaartemo (DSc, International Business) is Postdoctoral Researcher at Turku School of Economics, University of Turku, Finland. His research focuses on how emerging technologies shape market and societal practices.

Marius Kramer is the number one writer about bitcoin, cryptocurrencies and all things blockchain on Quora worldwide. Combined with a strong background in business, start-ups, computer science and AI, there are not many people like him with as much knowledge across all kinds of different cryptocurrencies, blockchain architectures and their tokenomics and market viability.

Pierluigi Martino is a PhD candidate in the Department of Economics and Management, University of Pisa. He has also been a research assistant at Cass Business School, City University of London. He is the author of research in the area of internal audit and risk management.

Thomas Mayer is Founding Director of the Flossbach von Storch Research Institute. Before this, he was Chief Economist of Deutsche Bank Group and head of DB Research. Thomas held positions at Goldman Sachs, Salomon Brothers and, before entering the private sector, the International Monetary Fund and the Kiel Institute of World Economics. Thomas received a doctoral degree in economics from Kiel University in 1982. Since 2003 and 2015, respectively, he is a CFA Charter holder and Honorary Professor at the University of Witten-Herdecke.

J. Mark Munoz is an MBA graduate and holds a PhD in Management. He is a tenured Full Professor of Management and International Business at Millikin University in Illinois and a former Visiting Fellow at the Kennedy School of Government at Harvard University. He is a recipient of several awards including four Best Research Paper Awards, two international book awards, a literary award and the ACBSP Teaching Excellence Award, among others. In 2016, he was recognized as the Distinguished Business Dean by the Academy of Global Business Advancement (AGBA). Aside from top-tier journal publications, he has authored/edited/coedited more than 20 books in management and economics such as *Winning across Borders*, *International Social Entrepreneurship*, *Handbook on the Geopolitics of Business*, *Managerial Forensics*, *Advances in Geoeconomics* and *Global Business Intelligence*. As Chairman/CEO of the international management consulting firm Munoz and Associates International, he directs and manages consulting projects worldwide.

Guych Nuryyev earned a PhD in Economics from Queen's University Belfast in 2011. He has taught at I-Shou University since then. His courses include "Economics of Cryptocurrency," the first full-semester course on the subject taught in Taiwan, among other finance classes.

Bruno Pasquier gained most of his law degrees from the University of Fribourg, Switzerland (Blaw 2008, Mlaw 2009, PhD 2014; Habilitation 2019);

he was admitted to the Swiss bar in 2011 and obtained an LL.M degree from UC Berkeley in 2018. He is currently Professor at the School of Management of Fribourg (HES-SO).

John E. Peterson earned a PhD in Finance from the University of Kansas in 1996, after which he joined Northern State University (NSU: Aberdeen, South Dakota, USA). His duties to NSU include teaching finance and economics related courses, research and service. He has published several articles in the area of derivative securities. Currently his research involves petroleum ETF market efficiency and cryptocurrencies. He has been presenting his research at various conferences, such as Academy of Business Research and International Association for Computer Information Systems.

David W. Savitski earned a PhD in Economics from UCLA in 1996, after which he taught economics at Northern State University (Aberdeen, South Dakota) for six years. He subsequently worked at the Federal Energy Regulatory Commission (Washington, D.C.) for 11 years. He recently retired from I-Shou University (Kaohsiung, Taiwan).

Hossein Sharif is a Fellow of the British Computer Society. He has nearly two decades of experience in digital technologies and ventures as a specialist, researcher, innovator, consultant, entrepreneur and executive. His involvement encompasses private, public and not-for-profit sectors in the UK, Europe and globally. Currently, he is the head of the Blockchain, Cryptocurrencies and FinTech (BCF) Research Group at the Newcastle Business School (UK). He is also engaged in research, consultancy and technology commercialization projects as well as providing education and training for executives and MBA and postgraduate candidates in the following fields, which also constitute his domains of research interest: blockchain and distributed autonomous systems, disruptive business models, FinTech, data science, process management and enterprise architecture.

Michael Woywode is Professor for SME Research and Entrepreneurship and the Director of the Institute for SME Research and Entrepreneurship at the University of Mannheim. His areas of expertise include business growth management, internationalization of high-tech start-ups and family business governance. He has published over 20 peer-reviewed articles, including some in *Academy of Management Journal and Organization Science*, as well as a number of books, policy studies and other scientific publications.

Evren Yazman is a member of the Blockchain, Cryptocurrencies and FinTech Research (BCF) Research Group at Newcastle Business School. His research interest lies in the applications of blockchain technology in finance. Evren is a CFA Charter holder and Qualified Financial Risk Manager.

Part I

Understanding cryptocurrencies

1 Cryptocurrencies in an economic context

An introduction

J. Mark Munoz and Michael Frenkel

Introduction

Cryptocurrencies are online protocols that serve as virtual currencies. The most famous cryptocurrency is bitcoin, which is based on a white paper published under the pseudonym "Satoshi Nakamoto" and which was launched in 2009. It aimed at creating digital money that would entail advantages that cash and other forms of currency do not offer. The notion of digital currency is not a new phenomenon. It was used in the 1990s through the use of value nodes through peer-to-peer payments (Clemons et al., 1996).

Cryptocurrencies have transformed the financial and economic terrain by reconfiguring the way money is transferred. Since the first cryptocurrency, bitcoin, was launched, it has become a global endeavor involving millions of individuals and organizations (Nakamoto, 2008; Hileman & Rauchs, 2017). Until mid-2016, the market of cryptocurrencies was not very dynamic, and total market capitalization was about USD 10 billion. A relatively short-lived hype in cryptocurrencies in 2017 led to a market capitalization that looked like a bubble with a peak at around USD 780 billion in January 2018. Although total market capitalization was down to USD 239 billion in mid-January 2020, the number of cryptocurrencies had increased significantly to more than 5,000 in 2020. However, most of the cryptocurrencies have a relatively low market capitalization. Bitcoin has by far the highest market capitalization (USD 158 billion), accounting for about two-thirds of the entire market (CoinMarketCap, 2020).

As Figure 1.1 shows, the market capitalization of bitcoin in early 2020 was only about half of what it was at the peak of the market in January 2018. However, average daily trading volume in early 2020 was about twice as high as in 2018.

The next most important cryptocurrencies are Etherium and Ripple with about ten and six percent of bitcoin's market share, respectively (Figure 1.2). The share of the next most important cryptocurrencies goes down very fast. The number 100 in the ranking of the cryptocurrencies of more than 5,000 different coins, accounting for 0.01 percent, and number 1,000, accounting for just 0.0003 percent. After the peak of the cryptocurrency market, market

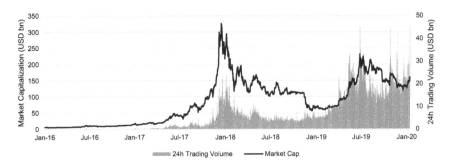

Figure 1.1 Bitcoin market capitalization and trading volume, 2016–2020

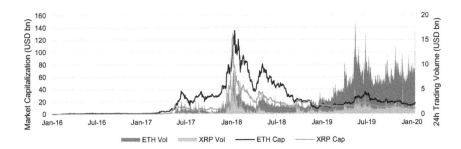

Figure 1.2 Etherium (ETH) and Ripple (XRP) market capitalization and trading volume, 2016–2020

capitalization of Etherium and Ripple, just like the vast majority of cryptocurrencies, declined much more than the market leader, bitcoin. However, their daily market volume has increased much more significantly than that of bitcoin.

The technological architecture of cryptocurrencies

The use of cryptocurrencies has been revolutionary. Cryptocurrencies like bitcoin represent a new form of digital currency that uses computer cryptology. It makes use of the blockchain technology applying distributed ledger technology. Ledgers comprise a number of standardized "blocks" that include information on the change of ownership and thus on transactions (Lansky, 2018).

Its basic structure is a decentralized authentication system and is thus independent of a central institution like a central bank. It appears useful to compare this structure with other payment structures. For example, paying cash requires the physical presence of the two parties involved. The ownership requires protection so that it is not stolen. Sending money within an electronic payment system uses a central institution checking the legitimacy of owners and payments and keeping records on accounts. Such a system uses a central authority to avoid the so-called double spending problem, which arises if transfer files can be copied several times. The central authority provides verification and confirmation. Such a payment system requires that participants trust the central authority to record the transactions and to manage the central ledger correctly. Nevertheless, this system can be subject to hacker attacks and technical failures. It also carries the risk of interference and confiscation of governments. By contrast, bitcoin does not use a central authority. Instead, there is a network, in which everyone can manage his or her own ledger.

Cryptocurrencies are available for trade. The most common form for an investor to enter the bitcoin system is to open an account with one of many existing bitcoin exchanges, to which fiat money can be sent and then exchanged in bitcoins. The system is anchored on a ledge system that collates balances using public keys. The method for making a transaction entails a person, say, the buyer of some products, who possesses a private key and broadcasts a message in a peer-to-peer network. This message informs the network that the bitcoin address of the seller of the products is the new owner of the bitcoins. The network validates the transaction in a public ledger and commits a block in the ledger. Evidence of work is often utilized to prevent tampering of the block. Each block points to another block, creating a so-called blockchain. Cryptocurrency miners seek to create a new block through solving a complex mathematical problem. The incentive for miners to find a solution is to collect a reward. This reward is predefined and in the bitcoin system consists of receiving newly created bitcoins through the new transaction. When a miner finds a new block, the block is broadcasted in the peer-to-peer network for other miners to validate and start the mining process for the next block. The ownership is recorded in multiple copies in the network. The mechanism of verifying and storing information about transactions to all nodes, i.e., the consensus mechanism, is the central innovation of the blockchain system.

The consensus mechanism representing an agreement on the transaction is called "proof of work." The number of participants in this peer-to-peer network is large, and every participant can remain anonymous (Berentsen & Schär, 2018). Even if the number of nodes increases or declines, the network is not endangered.

Contemporary economic features of cryptocurrencies

The cryptocurrency model has shifted financial transactions away from the use of central authorities (i.e., government institutions and banks) to the described system using cryptographic protocols. Cryptocurrencies set the stage for participation of millions of international and anonymous participants, thereby resulting in a profound economic impact.

At least ten attributes characterize cryptocurrencies in today's global economic environment:

Infancy: The cryptocurrency market is still in its early stages. The rate of its growth, usage and popularity will determine its future course.

Evolvement: The nature of cryptocurrencies has been evolving largely due to changes in market perception and participation.

Volatility: In recent years, the value of cryptocurrencies fluctuated heavily based on swings in market psychology and changes in supply and demand.

Inclusion: Buyers and sellers of cryptocurrencies span the globe. Participants in its global trading have included private individuals, investment houses and corporations across many countries.

Anonymity: Trading in cryptocurrency has been set up to keep trade transactions anonymous and confidential. The model prevents any entity from monitoring or blocking movements of funds.

Legitimacy: The blockchain model supporting cryptocurrency creation has been created to optimize security and legitimacy of transactions.

Energy: Mining of cryptocurrencies such as bitcoin requires the use of a lot of energy. Energy costs factors heavily into the viability of cryptocurrency mining.

Location: Since energy costs vary across locations, cost of bitcoin mining varies from one location to another. Locations with lower energy costs tend to be more attractive to cryptocurrency miners.

Technology: The creation and mining of cryptocurrency requires a significant level of technological competencies. Individuals and organizations that have a strong technological foundation can gain a unique competitive advantage.

No oversight: Given the emphasis on privacy and security in cryptocurrency transactions, there is a lack of oversight and control of trading processes. Illegitimate as well as legitimate participation in the cryptocurrency ecosystem elevates transaction risk despite the sustainability of the model as a whole.

In the economic realm, these attributes suggest that countries differ in their ability to develop cryptocurrencies within the country or even to actively participate in cryptocurrency trading. Given the reliance on certain skills, technological infrastructure and government policies, there exist a variation worldwide in cryptocurrency usage across countries. The depth of the economic impact of cryptocurrencies therefore differs from one country to another.

Are cryptocurrencies money?

If cryptocurrencies function as money, they can have a significant impact on investment, consumption, money supply, prices and the development of wealth (Selgin, 2014). However, are cryptocurrencies money? Economists typically refer to the standard three functions of money: (1) money as a medium of exchange, (2) money as a unit of account and (3) money as a store of value. In order for cryptocurrencies to become a medium of exchange, one must be able use them to buy goods or assets. Common acceptance, low costs of transactions, divisibility, stability and protection from counterfeiting are among the prerequisites for a good medium of exchange, which increase the efficiency of the economy. While fiat money fulfills these conditions in most countries, bitcoin and other cryptocurrencies fulfill them to a much lesser extent. There are indications that bitcoin has mainly served as a medium of exchange for illicit purposes (Foley et al., 2018). As for other payments, the fact that cryptocurrencies have no intrinsic value and have shown high price volatility vis-à-vis other currencies has especially limited the willingness of economic agents to accept them as media of exchange. While some merchants and institutions have begun to accept bitcoins as a means of payment, such cases have so far been more of an exception. Other problems in this context are that transactions are costly because digital wallets are expensive to maintain and obtaining bitcoins is not as easy as obtaining fiat money (Yermack, 2015).

Money as a unit of account reflects that it is widely used as a numéraire to quote prices and thereby indicate the value of goods and assets. This function is important in the decision making about buying and selling and is therefore crucial for enabling and smoothing trade and investment. The main prerequisite for this function of money is stability because only then can economic agents design sensible financial plans and assess the value of goods and assets over time. In the context of bitcoin, another problem is that merchants who want to quote prices of ordinary goods in bitcoin have to do this out to four or five decimal places with several zeros at the beginning, which is very unusual. In essence, bitcoin and other cryptocurrencies have hardly fulfilled this function of money largely because of their price fluctuations.

In order for cryptocurrencies to become a store of value, economic agents must be willing to accumulate wealth in them. Prerequisites for anything to provide the function of store of value include durability, scarcity, stability, protection, low storage cost, exchangeability and liquidity. These prerequisites help enable efficient allocation of resources. Bitcoin and other cryptocurrencies have been more successful in serving this function of money than the other functions. Therefore, some researchers view cryptocurrencies more as a financial investment closer to a stock than to a currency (Glaser et al., 2014). However, despite the objective of the bitcoin system to provide a safe network, there have been cases in which bitcoins were stolen by hackers or bitcoin exchanges. In addition, in the course of the bankruptcy of Japanese-based Mt. Gox, 754,000 were lost, worth around USD 450 million (Böhme et al., 2015). Bitcoin and other cryptocurrencies have assumed some store of value function, driven partly by speculation during the hype in 2017.

Cryptocurrencies: the pros and cons

Several advantages and disadvantages are associated with cryptocurrencies within a business and economic paradigm. As the construction of cryptocurrencies differ somewhat, affecting advantages and disadvantages, we here focus on bitcoin. Its advantages include the following (Rogojanu & Badea, 2014):

- Transactions provide business flexibility because they can be made from anywhere and at any point in time.
- Bitcoin provides scarcity, which contributes to their value.
- Bitcoin does not create inflation.
- Despite some exceptional circumstances that have occurred, bitcoin provides a high level of security.
- Bitcoin provides confidentiality and anonymity.
- Bitcoin is independent of a central authority such as a central bank and government.

While these advantages are quite compelling, significant disadvantages exist (Böhme et al., 2015):

- Price developments have displayed excessive volatility in recent years, implying very high market risk.
- Bitcoin and other cryptocurrencies can be subject to speculative attacks.
- There is transaction risk, as transactions are irreversible and cannot be tracked in case of mistakes.
- There is significant investment in energy generation costs, making it difficult to participate in the market.
- It creates incentives for illegal activities such as drugs, money laundering and tax evasion, as it reduces the risk of getting caught.
- As many agents use bitcoin exchanges, which function like banks, to facilitate participation in the bitcoin market, there is counterparty risk involving the collapse of such institutions. If agents alternatively use digital wallet services, there is cybercrime risk involving fraud. In essence, there is no consumer protection.
- There is operational risk resulting from possible security flaws and malware (Weaver, 2018).
- The long-term viability of the cryptocurrency model remains in question because there are issues such as cryptographic challenges and the system security, among others (Eyal & Sirer, 2014).
- Bitcoin is not completely anonymous. There is a user identifier, although without names.
- There are several legal and regulatory risks including uncertain tax treatment of bitcoin profit and losses (Bryans, 2014). There are also the first signs of the possibility of regulatory oversight.
- Cryptocurrencies have repercussions in the political, sociological and ethical realms (Karlstrøm, 2014; Maurer et al., 2013; Krugman, 2013).

The discussed pros and cons highlight the fact that there remains a lack of clarity on the strength of cryptocurrencies as a form of currency or investment. Given that monetary or investment values are largely shaped by market psychology, the opportunities and risks associated with cryptocurrencies remain unclear. Furthermore, given the hazards of an unregulated environment, in which cryptocurrencies operate and their growing significant impact on the economies of some countries, there is some merit associated with the creation of an International Cryptocurrency Board to provide some oversight in the industry.

Emergence of cryptocurrencies and book structure

With the growing interest and heightened economic participation of cryptocurrencies on the world stage, the study of this topic will likely increase in the coming years. This book aims at capturing diverse viewpoints on cryptocurrencies and at examining its economic impact in our contemporary society.

The content is beneficial to academics as they endeavor to expand research and understanding of the subject. The topic is useful to managers and entrepreneurs in their efforts toward understanding the business implications of cryptocurrencies. Consultants, international organizations and government policy makers will find the insights helpful in the understanding of the challenges and opportunities brought about by the use of cryptocurrencies.

The book has three parts and 12 chapters: **Part I: Understanding cryptocurrencies** – (1) Cryptocurrencies in an economic context: an introduction (*J. Mark Munoz and Michael Frenkel*), (2) Understanding the distinctive features of cryptocurrencies (*Valtteri Kaartemo and Marius Kramer*), (3) Categorization of Cryptoassets (*Evren Yazamn and Hossein Sharif*), (4) The economic nature of bitcoin: money, new gold or speculative assets? (*Silvia Dal Bianco*), (5) The microeconomics of cryptocurrencies (*Guych Nuryyev, David W. Savitski and John E. Peterson*).

Part II: Cryptocurrencies in industry – (6) The sources of cybersecurity threats in cryptocurrency (*Valtteri Kaartemo and Marius Kramer*), (7) Cryptocurrencies and entrepreneurial finance (*Pierluigi Martino, Cristiano Bellavitis and Carlos M. DaSilva*), (8) Crowdfunding and initial coin offerings (*Jean-Marie Ayer and Bruno Pasquier*), (9) Cryptocurrencies and trade (*Allison Derrick*).

Part III: Political and economic implications of cryptocurrencies – (10) Central bank digital currency: aims, mechanisms and macroeconomic impact (*Silvia Dal Bianco*), (11) Crypto money and cryptocurrency competition (*Björn Holste and Thomas Mayer*), (12) The geoeconomics of cryptocurrencies: an institutional perspective (*Andrew Isaak, Suleika Bort and Michael Woywode*).

As one of the pioneering and most comprehensive books on the subject, the editors hope that this endeavor encourages thorough research on the subject. It is also hoped that this book stimulates the creation of new business ideas and economic models that could positively transform our global society through the efficient and responsible use of cryptocurrencies.

References

Berentsen, A., and Schär, F. (2018). A short introduction to the world of cryptocurrencies. *Federal Reserve Bank of St. Louis Review*, 100 (1), 1–16.

Böhme, R., Christin, N., Edelman, B., and Moore, T. (2015). Bitcoin: Economics, technology, and governance. *Journal of Economic Perspectives*, 29 (2), 213–238.

Bryans, D. (2014). Bitcoin and money laundering: Mining for an effective solution. *Indiana Law Journal*, 89 (1), 441–472.

Clemons, E. K., Croson, D. C., and Weber, B. W. (1996). Reengineering money: The Mondex stored value card and beyond. *International Journal of Electronic Commerce*, 1 (2), 5–31.

CoinMarketCap. (2020). *Total Market Capitalization*. Retrieved January 15, 2020, from http://www.coinmarketcap.com/all/views/all/ and from https://coinmarketcap.com/charts/.

Eyal, I., and Sirer, E. G. (2014). Majority is not enough: Bitcoin mining is vulnerable. In N. Christin and R. Safavi-Naini (eds.), *Lecture Notes in Computer Science 8437* (pp. 436–454). Berlin, Heidelberg: Springer.

Foley, S., Karlsen, J. R., and Putniņš, T. J. (2018). Sex, drugs, and Bitcoin: How much illegal activity is financed through cryptocurrency? *Review of Financial Studies*, 32 (5), 1798–1853.

Glaser, F., Zimmermann, K., Haferkorn, M., and Weber, M. C. (2014). Bitcoin: Asset or currency? Revealing users' hidden intentions. In M. Avital, J. M. Leimeister and U. Schultze (eds.), *Proceedings of the 22nd European Conference on Information Systems*. Tel Aviv: Association for Information Systems.

Hileman, G., and Rauchs, M. (2017). *Global Cryptocurrency Benchmarking Study*. Cambridge: Centre for Alternative Finance Global Cryptocurrency Benchmarking Study.

Karlstrøm, H. (2014). Do libertarians dream of electric coins? The material embeddedness of Bitcoin, Distinktion. *Scandinavian Journal of Social Theory*, 15 (1), 23–36.

Krugman, P. (2013). Bitcoin is evil. *New York Times*, December 28.

Lansky, J. (2018). Possible state approaches to cryptocurrencies. *Journal of Systems Integration*, 9 (1), 19–31.

Maurer, B., Nelms, T. C., and Swartz, L. (2013). When perhaps the real problem is money itself! The practical materiality of Bitcoin. *Social Semiotics*, 23 (2), 261–277.

Nakamoto, S. (2008). *Bitcoin: A Peer-to-Peer Electronic Cash System*. Retrieved November 14, 2018, from http://bitcoin.org/bitcoin.pdf.

Rogojanu, A., and Badea, L. (2014). The issue of competing currencies. *Case Study – Bitcoin, Theoretical and Applied Economics*, 21 (1), 103–114.

Selgin, G. (2014). Synthetic commodity money. *Journal of Financial Stability*, 17, 92–99.

Weaver, N. (2018). Risks of cryptocurrencies. *Communications of the ACM*, 61 (6), 20–24.

Yermack, D. (2013). Is Bitcoin a real currency? An economic appraisal. *Handbook of Digital Currency*, 2015, 31–43.

2   Understanding the distinctive features of cryptocurrencies

Valtteri Kaartemo and Marius Kramer

Introduction

If one has followed the business news over the past decade, it has been challenging to not notice the increasing interest in cryptocurrencies. However, what may still remain surprising – even to the readers of this book – is the vast number of various cryptocurrencies available. In fact, more than 5,000 cryptocurrencies (including coins and tokens) are already featured in Coinmarketcap.com as of early 2020. Moreover, while many might be able to name bitcoin, Ethereum and Ripple's XRP, their distinctive features against one another and various alternative cryptocurrencies (altcoins) are less known beyond a selected group of cryptocurrency experts.

This chapter briefly describes the basics of cryptocurrencies and discusses their main distinctive features. We build on the extant academic literature and our practical experience on the theme to provide a framework for assessing cryptocurrencies consisting of six criteria that are required in order to become a global currency that can serve 5 billion people using it ten times a day and is secure against nearly all attacks. We show with illustrative examples how the framework can be used for understanding different cryptocurrencies. We use the framework for showing some of the limitations of the top ten cryptocurrencies on market capitalization (for reference, see coinmarketcap.com) and introduce handpicked projects beyond the top ten that meet all the criteria. Of note, the framework is not meant as financial advice. Rather, it can be used for understanding the differences in the technical design of cryptocurrencies. Also, other projects can meet all the criteria but could not be included due to space limitations.

To introduce our framework, we systematically refer to bitcoin, as it is the most mature and the biggest cryptocurrency in the market (as of early 2020). In other words, we use bitcoin as an illustrative example of how the technical features of cryptocurrencies may be compared against one another. Thus, it is not our intention to downgrade bitcoin as a payment system by illuminating some of its technical limitations. Moreover, it is not the intent of this chapter to describe the complete bitcoin system. Interested readers can refer to Nakamoto's (2008) white paper or Antonopoulos's (2014) book for a more extended description of bitcoin.

As a practical implication, our criteria can be used to understand the differences between bitcoin and other cryptocurrencies. While neither the book chapter nor the criteria should be interpreted as investment advice, we expect it to help both novice and more experienced cryptocurrency enthusiasts to do their own research on what cryptocurrencies they should buy and use for various purposes.

Framework for assessing the distinctive features of cryptocurrencies

Our framework consists of six criteria. In the following discussion, we will introduce the criteria and then use the framework for comparing the top ten cryptocurrencies.

1. Near infinite scalability

That means they are able to process at least millions of transactions per second and possibly also billions. The scalability is clearly an issue with bitcoin, and the bitcoin community has debated about different ways to make it more scalable. The problem is that bitcoin was designed in a way that a ledger registers all system transactions. As per its own design, this leads to the constant increase of the blockchain. Consequently, the system has faced problems of scalability, and it is expected to face even bigger ones. These issues are latency and bootstrap time that define the efficiency of the payment system (Croman et al., 2016). Briefly, the maximum size of blocks has limited the size of a bitcoin block to 1 MB. Consequently, this allows only seven transactions per second, which does not allow the system to be used even close to the magnitude of credit cards today, i.e., 50,000 per second (Herrera-Joancomartí & Pérez-Solà, 2016). While a solution could be provided through off-chain payment channels (transaction not showing up on a public ledger), this may cause some trouble in terms of privacy (Herrera-Joancomartí & Pérez-Solà, 2016).

2. Near infinite decentralization

Wang et al. (2018) divides blockchains into three categories: public, consortium and private. In these blockchains, consensus is determined by all miners (public), selected sets of nodes (consortium) or a single organization (private). As a result, centralization varies from decentralized (public) to partially centralized (consortium) and fully centralized (private). Bitcoin was originally designed as a decentralized, public currency that uses proof of work (PoW) as a consensus strategy. In brief, all participants of the PoW process ("miners") have to calculate the hash value of a block, and once a node obtains the relevant value, all other nodes validate the correctness of the value to avoid frauds. The idea is that instead of central banks validating transactions, a distributed consensus mechanism spreads the votes and decision power among several different nodes across the globe (Wang et al., 2018). By design, this means that the process is highly decentralized.

Although bitcoin was designed as a decentralized system, over the years it has become more and more centralized as the mining process has been concentrated among few very large mining pools. In fact, the reports (blockchain.com, 2019) show that the four largest mining pools (BTC.com, F2Pool, Poolin and AntPool) together control more than 51 percent (as a "rough estimate") of the total hash power of the bitcoin network. This makes bitcoin relatively centralized as well as potentially vulnerable to 51 percent attacks (Bradbury, 2013), although it is not easy to attack the largest companies. Moreover, a significant share of bitcoins are still stored in centralized exchanges. Interestingly, also the development is relatively centralized, as bitcoin's governance is controlled by only two companies, Chaincode Labs and Blockstream, which make more than 51 percent of the github commits (Reddit, 2018), i.e., saved changes on GitHub.

3. *Permissionlessness and trustlessness*

This feature is closely linked with centralization. Permissionlessness means that there is no third party making rules about how to vote, thus giving permission to operate in the system. Trustlessness means that nodes do not need to trust one another in order to participate in the voting. If one of the parties gives permissions, the system easily becomes a victim of cartel formation, lobbying and blackmailing. When all parties are equal, there is no room for social engineering in the system, and the system is more probably fair to each node.

While bitcoin was designed as a permissionless and trustless system, Vidan and Lehdonvirta (2019, p. 44) have criticized that there is "a persistent gap between this goal of trustlessness and its practical operations." For instance, peer production of the code for bitcoin should result in a fair code, but as some companies or organizations may be more active in development, there is a challenge of uneven dynamics of peer production.

4. *Low energy usage*

The PoW design has resulted in a situation that mining is not only centralized but very energy intensive. First, when bitcoin mining gained popularity, CPUs became inefficient, as graphics hardware (GPU) was added to increase the hash power of desktop computers. When the difficulty of bitcoin mining and the price soared, the miners started to construct mining farms – a combination of Application-Specific Integrated Circuits (ASIC) that are specifically designed for mining bitcoin (O'Dwyert & Malone, 2014). The use of large ASIC mining farms and GPUs causes not only a rise in the economic cost but the environmental burden of bitcoin mining. As a result, we have witnessed calls for more sustainable development of block-chain technologies (Truby, 2018).

Currently bitcoin uses more than 70 TWh per year, around the electricity equivalent of Austria. While the exact energy use of the bitcoin system is debated, there is a general consensus that it is unsustainable. Particularly if bitcoin gains in popularity, the energy use is about to skyrocket, making bitcoin unusable as a global currency. Consequently, it is considered that legal and policy tools are required for moving toward the use of ASIC- and GPU-resistant cryptocurrencies.

5. Near instant transactions

One of the main issues for bitcoin has been the long transaction time and that has led to several forks (splits in the blockchain) aiming at solving the problem. While slow transaction time might be acceptable for a cryptocurrency that is store of value (commodity), it is not possible to use this kind of cryptocurrencies in regular payments. For instance, with bitcoin, it can take several minutes to send and receive coins. And when the system congests, it can take several hours to get a transaction confirmed. As a result, businesses and individuals need to think about whether they can risk the reduction in service experience due to slow transaction time (Hughes et al., 2019).

For practical use in supermarkets and the like, transactions should be confirmed within seconds. For many use cases, 10 seconds is already too much. This would add much overhead and a lot of lost revenue to any retailer or supermarket. Naturally, this is context dependent, and for some transactions a 10-second wait is acceptable. For instance, when making big purchases like buying a house, a car or machinery in an industrial setting, buyers and sellers are willing to accept slower transactions. The technology for this already exists in blockchains like Nano, Elastos, Quarkchain and Zilliqa, which can reach thousands of transactions per second (TPS) while having near infinite decentralization.

6. Zero fees

For smaller transactions, it is also important that the cost of transaction is low. In order to become more mainstream, cryptocurrency transactions cannot be much more than credit card fees or the cost of handling cash at the register. While large transaction fees attract miners to partake in the blockchain and enable the viability of cryptocurrency, high fees potentially guide users toward other cryptocurrencies and fiat money (Easley et al., 2019).

When transaction time increases, there is a tendency for transaction fees also to go up. This is because senders try to incentivize bitcoin miners to prefer the confirmation of their transaction. As a result, a single transaction can cost several dollars in fiat equivalent. For instance, on December 21, 2017, the transaction fee for confirmation within 6 blocks (in an hour) rose above USD 35 per transaction. This makes the transfer of small amounts of bitcoin temporarily economically unsustainable.

A comparison of cryptocurrencies with the framework

The preceding criteria may be used to highlight the differences among the top ten cryptocurrencies (by market capitalization). For instance, some other top cryptocurrencies are more scalable than bitcoin; specifically, EOS can handle nearly 3,000 TPS compared to bitcoin's 7 TPS (Hughes et al., 2019). On the other hand, while bitcoin may be viewed as centralized, Ripple's XRP is claimed by many to be much more centralized, as a single entity controls a majority of the voting power.

The framework may also be used for analyzing the differences among altcoins. In other words, you may be able to find cryptocurrencies that are scalable, decentralized, permissionless, low in energy consumption, fast and inexpensive to transact.

For instance, VeriCoin & Verium scores high in all these features with its unique design combining proof-of-work time (PoWT) with proof-of-stake time (PoST). It is the first dual blockchain protocol that pairs a digital currency (VeriCoin, PoST) with a digital commodity (Verium, PoWT) that forms a binary chain (VeriCoin & Verium – Official Site, 2020). Thus, it is possible to achieve scalability and fast transactions without compromising on security and centralization. It is also ASIC and GPU resistant, which makes it energy efficient compared to many other PoW cryptocurrency projects.

Conclusion

The purpose of this chapter is to increase our understanding of the distinctive features of cryptocurrencies. This is important as we already have more than 5,000 different cryptocurrencies in circulation. We focus on six main features, which help comparing different cryptocurrencies, namely scalability, centralization, permissionlessness, energy consumption, transaction time and transaction fees. We show that, in these terms, bitcoin, the clear leader in market capitalization, is not strongly positioned against other top cryptocurrencies. Moreover, we are able to use the template to reveal some challengers beyond the top ten that have a distinctive design in terms of these features (without compromising in any feature).

Of note, the chapter focuses on the features that relate to the technical design of the cryptocurrencies. We agree that the social aspects of cryptocurrencies could also be used to distinguish coins from one another. For instance, we argue that the number of monthly average users is an important key metric in understanding how widely the cryptocurrency has spread and indicates that the coin is actually used. The use cases are important, as many coins may be technologically advanced but never gain traction. Here, a look at the size and capability of the team is also important, as well as the quality of marketing.

However, while we could have adopted a more sociotechnical viewpoint on highlighting the distinctive features of cryptocurrencies, we feel that, in the market coming of age, the focus should still rely on understanding the differences on the technical side. Particularly in 2017, hundreds of cryptocurrencies backed by an initial coin offering (ICO) appeared, raised millions of dollars and ended up having massive marketing programs without the ability to deliver technologically distinctive solutions.

At the end, we would like to underline that we do not give any investment advice in this chapter. Instead, we encourage people to do their own research and make their own decisions about whether they truly feel comfortable engaging in a centralized project or buying decentralized coins that are not as widely used but provide a technically unique design. We hope that increasing understanding of the important technological features helps to illuminate the best projects among hundreds of badly designed cryptocurrencies, and people – new and more experienced – can make more justified decisions about which cryptocurrencies they buy and use.

References

Antonopoulos, A. (2014). *Mastering Bitcoins*. Sebastopol, CA: O'Reilly.

Bradbury, D. (2013). The problem with Bitcoin. *Computer Fraud and Security*, 2013 (11), 5–8. https://doi.org/10.1016/S1361-3723(13)70101-5.

Croman, K., Decker, C., Eyal, I., Efe Gencer, A., Juels, A., Kosba, A., . . . Wattenhofer, R. (2016). On scaling decentralized blockchains initiative for cryptocurrencies and contracts (IC3). *International Conference on Financial Cryptography and Data Security*, 106–125. Retrieved from http://fc16.ifca.ai/bitcoin/papers/CDE+16.pdf.

Easley, D., O'Hara, M., and Basu, S. (2019). From mining to markets: The evolution of Bitcoin transaction fees. *Journal of Financial Economics*, 134 (1), 91–109. https://doi.org/10.1016/j.jfineco.2019.03.004.

Herrera-Joancomartí, J., and Pérez-Solà, C. (2016). Privacy in Bitcoin transactions: New challenges from blockchain scalability solutions. In V. Torra, Y. Narukawa, G. Navarro-Arribas, and C. Yañez (eds.), *Modeling Decisions for Artificial Intelligence. MDAI 2016. Lecture Notes in Computer Science* (Vol. 9880, pp. 26–44). Cham: Springer. https://doi.org/10.1007/978-3-319-45656-0_3.

Hughes, A., Park, A., Kietzmann, J., and Archer-Brown, C. (2019). Beyond Bitcoin: What blockchain and distributed ledger technologies mean for firms. *Business Horizons*. https://doi.org/10.1016/j.bushor.2019.01.002.

Nakamoto, S. (2008). *Bitcoin: A Peer-to-Peer Electronic Cash System*. Retrieved from https://bitcoin.org/bitcoin.pdf.

O'Dwyert, K. J., and Malone, D. (2014). Bitcoin mining and its energy footprint. *IET Conference Publications*, 2014 (CP639), 280–285. https://doi.org/10.1049/cp.2014.0699.

Reddit. (2018). Debunking: "Blockstream is 3 or 4 developers out of hundreds of developers at Core" – Tone Vays. Retrieved from www.reddit.com/r/btc/comments/7lio87/debunking_blockstream_is_3_or_4_developers_out_of/.

Truby, J. (2018). Decarbonizing Bitcoin: Law and policy choices for reducing the energy consumption of Blockchain technologies and digital currencies. *Energy Research and Social Science*, 44, July, 399–410. https://doi.org/10.1016/j.erss.2018.06.009.

VeriCoin & Verium – Official Site. (2020). Retrieved January 9, 2020, from https://veri-coin.info/.

Vidan, G., and Lehdonvirta, V. (2019). Mine the gap: Bitcoin and the maintenance of trustlessness. *New Media and Society*, 21 (1), 42–59. https://doi.org/10.1177/1461444818786220.

Wang, H., Zheng, Z., Xie, S., Dai, H. N., and Chen, X. (2018). Blockchain challenges and opportunities: A survey. *International Journal of Web and Grid Services*, 14 (4), 352. https://doi.org/10.1504/ijwgs.2018.10016848.

3 Categorization of cryptoassets[1]

Evren Yazman and Hossein Sharif

Introduction

Bitcoin was the first cryptocurrency and introduced a technology that allows peer-to-peer transfer of an asset without going through a financial institution (Nakamoto, 2008). This technology of a universal distributed ledger that allows a value to be recorded, verified and cryptographically secured without requiring a trusted third party is now known as the blockchain, or more broadly as distributed ledger technology (DLT).

Many other cryptocurrencies followed, and the number of users have grown especially rapidly since 2016 (Figure 3.1).

While the user base still represents a very small percentage of the world population, the term "crypto" has risen in popularity especially amongst the young generations (Figure 3.2).

Currently, over 5,000 "cryptocurrencies" are listed on popular websites (*All Cryptocurrencies | CoinMarketCap*, 2020). Such a long list hides a lot of variation among the names on the list and makes it very difficult for newcomers to get an understanding of this universe.

Especially younger generations, who do not have much prior experience with financial markets and are considering crypto as an investment, may find it difficult to assess the differences. It is therefore essential that we classify these assets into some basic categories, or "cryptoasset classes," in a manner that is consistent with how financial assets are typically classified.

In this chapter, we define all types of assets that are recorded on a blockchain as "cryptoassets" (House of Commons Treasury Comittee, 2018). We then use the classification of regulators (*Firms That Need Authorisation | FCA*, 2020; *SEC. gov | Framework for "Investment Contract" Analysis of Digital Assets*, n.d.), as well as practitioner-accepted terminology (Sharma, 2019), to define the broad categories.

This leads us to three main categories of cryptoassets:

1 *Cryptocurrencies*: A currency is money used as a unit of account and means of exchange in an economy. Cryptocurrencies are currencies that are recorded on a blockchain and that aim to perform the money function.
2 *Utility tokens*: Utility tokens are blockchain-based assets that allow holders to use a blockchain application or that gives them some other tangible or intangible benefit.

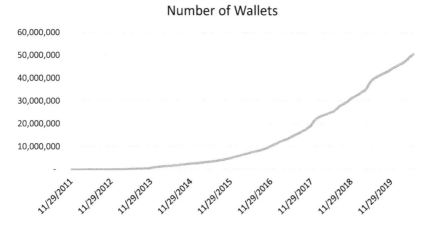

Figure 3.1 Number of blockchain wallet users

Source: Blockchain.com (*Blockchain Charts – The Total Number of Unique Blockchain.com Wallets Created*, 2020)

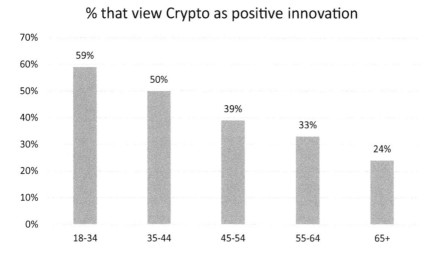

Figure 3.2 Percentage of age group that view bitcoin as a positive innovation in financial technology

Source: Blockchain Capital (Bogart, 2019)

3   *Security tokens*: Securities are investment products that one invests in to get future financial gains. Security tokens are such investments represented digitally and registered on a blockchain.

Each of these categories has a fundamentally different function. Economically they come with different financial risks and rewards that are inherent based on their category.

We will start this chapter with a history of the blockchain in order to give some background as to how these different cryptoassets have emerged. We will identify the gap in existing categorizations and explain why a more detailed study is required. Finally, we will provide some more details in each category and any subcategories. This chapter aims to outline financial characteristics of different cryptoasset categories and help users better asses the risks and uses for each asset.

Evolution of cryptoassets

The concept of digital money has been around since the 1980s, but a decentralized and secure digital money became a reality only with the bitcoin (Tschorsch & Scheuermann, 2016). Bitcoin created a representation of a value on a digital ledger, which was the bitcoin blockchain. This value could be exchanged on a peer-to-peer basis and recorded on the blockchain securely. It was designed to be a peer to peer payment service and to replace other currencies as a way for transfers. Unlike traditional banknotes, cryptocurrencies have no tangible existence; rather they are electronic signals, and records that keep track of transactions mediated with the currency and are not legal tender, i.e., recognized by a specific legal system (Smith & Kumar, 2018).

Later different distributed ledgers have been established with similar technological principles, each having a native "cryptocurrency" that can be exchanged between parties on that ledger. Although each of these ledgers and currencies may have had slightly different technological features or economic principles, they were still aiming to be used as a payment method. The introduction of Ethereum created a new type of use for the distributed ledgers. Ethereum was designed to be a world computer that could process transactions in a decentralized and secure manner, hence it opened up the possibility for exchange of different values through smart contracts (Davidson et al., 2018). Ethereum was the native cryptocurrency of the Ethereum blockchain; however, in addition to its ability for peer-to-peer transfer, it was also necessary to pay for processing of transactions on the Ethereum blockchain. This function created a second category for cryptoassets that were to be used as "utility tokens" to get services on a specific blockchain. Ethereum also made it possible for any user to create "tokens" on Ethereum blockchain. These tokens could then be utilized to buy services on protocols or applications that were being built on top of Ethereum blockchain or elsewhere, expanding the universe of tokens (Rohr & Wright, 2017). This led to many groups or projects issuing tokens through initial coin offerings (ICOs) to raise money for their projects and to public buying of these tokens with the expectation of their value increasing over time. Although these tokens were commonly referred to as "cryptocurrencies," they did not all fall into the previous two categories, i.e., they were not designed to facilitate peer–to-peer payments or to buy services on a platform. Some of them were used to organize governance of the protocol, to give voting rights, rights to participate in a certain protocol, and in some cases to share in future returns. As a combination of these factors made these instruments more similar to equities, this third category caught the attention of regulators. Regulators provided some guidelines that, regardless of the format, whether it is recorded on a blockchain or in a traditional format, assets with certain characteristics will be considered securities. This has significantly reduced the number of ICOs. However, it has also confirmed that the third category of cryptoassets, which are regulated investment products that are registered on public blockchains, is possible (*Cryptoassets Taskforce: Final Report*, 2018).

As these assets came into existence over time, they were simply added to an ever increasing list. They have been typically classified according to their differentiating technological characteristics or the problems they are trying to solve.

Asset categorization

As more people started to look at crypto as an alternative investment class, it is crucial to apply a financial classification to these assets that goes beyond their technical classification. In finance, it is a basic principle to classify assets based on their economic substance and risk–return characteristics. Assets are firstly grouped into broad asset classes such as fixed income, equities, commodities and currencies. There are also various subcategories within each asset class. It would be nonsensical to compare the total money supply of an emerging market country and the market capitalization of a U.S. stock to each other, but that is effectively how the crypto market lists have mostly been compared to date. This causes a lot of confusion and misconceptions.

First, all assets recorded on a blockchain tend to be called "cryptocurrency" among the public. In this chapter, we want to establish that these should be more aptly called "cryptoassets." Cryptocurrencies are only one of the categories of cryptoassets. While the value of cryptocurrencies may fluctuate, it is important to also know that holding one currency versus another is not an "investment" in the traditional sense, it is merely speculation on its future value. An investment is use of a currency in an activity to accrue future returns.

The second category of utility tokens are like the commodities within the cryptoassets. Typically there is no inherent return to holding a commodity other than its utility value. The price of commodities is therefore driven by supply and demand for that commodity, as well as some factors that can impact their pricing such as storage and transfer costs or interest rates.

The third category is the security tokens. Any asset that is being offered for investment purposes and gives some rights over future returns will in fact be classified under this section and will be subject to regulation. This is the area where a lot of innovation may be expected to happen that will impact the financial markets.

In this section we investigate each of these categories further.

1. Cryptocurrencies

The first category only aims to have a currency function; they aim to be used as money in the economy. Although money itself may not be a regulated investment, financial services that involve the transfer or safekeeping of money are typically regulated (*Firms That Need Authorisation | FCA*, 2020). We will not go into much detail about this category in this chapter, as this will be the focus of most other chapters in this book. The concerns in implementation of any of these and the challenges of such projects are beyond the remit of this chapter. We will instead highlight some of the subcategories within this category.

Decentralized cryptocurrencies. The main characteristic of these currencies is their decentralized nature. They aim to replace fiat currencies issued by central authorities by bringing an uncontrolled alternative. Bitcoin is the first and most widely known of such currencies. It is based on a concept of limited supply, which is where it is expected to derive its value from. There have been many clones of this setup, each of which aim to bring some technological advancement to bitcoin to differentiate itself, whether it be the scalability, processing speed, privacy and so on.

There are a number of challenges on the wider adoption of these currencies, both from the technical and the regulatory perspectives (Morisse, 2015; Holub & Johnson, 2018; Nelson, 2018).

Central bank digital currencies (CBDCs). This is the other extreme. They will be issued by central banks, which are the existing issuers of fiat currencies. It is just a digital representation of the currency and should become part of the money supply. A number of central banks are working on this around the world at different stages of development (Meaning et al., 2018; Carney, 2018; Yao, 2018).

Stable coins. As decentralized currencies fluctuate a lot in value, they have not been acceptable for most real-world uses as a valid currency. Also, since no major CBDC is available, other initiatives have been formed to create stable coins that can be used for transactions on blockchain. The first category of these are linked to a specific fiat currency (such as Tether, which is USD in a bank account wrapped in blockchain token). These tokens are issued by the sponsor on a private or public blockchain and can be used to facilitate transactions that need to be denominated in the fiat currency. The second category consists of algorithmic stable coins; these may be backed by other crypto collateral that gets rebalanced to keep a peg to a fiat currency (e.g., DAI) and in some experiments are not backed by an asset but rather aims to create a decentralized digital currency for which the stability of the value will be ensured through algorithms that control supply/demand dynamics (e.g., basis coin).

Asset-backed coins. The final category can be seen as an extension of stable coins. Instead of being backed by a single fiat currency, these are backed by other pools of assets. The first group of these were backed by commodities, such as gold (e.g., DigiX) or oil. Such commodities have historically been used as mediums of exchange or units of account. Having them digitally represented makes their transfer much simpler; therefore it is a natural extension to have digital currencies backed by such commodities. The second group uses a basket of fiat currencies and financial instruments to back a new currency. This is similar to the concept of SDR (special drawing rights) of the International Monetary Fund (IMF), which is used as a unit of account for transactions with multilateral organizations, as well as certain international contracts and payments. The project that got most attention in this category is Libra of Facebook, probably because of the extent of the reach of its sponsor (Carney, 2019).

2. Utility tokens

The first wave of blockchains were single purpose and were designed for peer-to-peer money transfer. The second wave, starting with Ethereum, saw ever increasing developments on the protocol layer, which made it easier to build apps for various uses of blockchain. These protocols had their native tokens, which were needed to participate and to get the service from the specific protocol. Ether, used by Ethereum, was the first such token. It is used to get transactions processed on a distributed world computer, and it has also been used as the reference currency for all other projects that were built on top of Ethereum. It is therefore sometimes considered a hybrid of cryptocurrency and a utility token. These tokens can therefore be likened to commodities, which are specific inputs that need to be used for the production of certain output. It is also no coincidence that the utility token used on Ethereum network is called "Gas," which is probably the first utility token and is a clear reference to a commodity. Gas in Ethereum fuels the ability to execute transactions on the Ethereum networks, just like oil and gas fuel production in the physical world. The commodities do not exist for the purpose of being a financial product, but their prices fluctuate by their supply and demand dynamics. Regulators therefore do not regulate commodity markets and have also kept utility tokens outside the regulation as long as they meet certain criteria (*Cryptoassets Taskforce: Final Report*, 2018).

There are various economic and operating models for utility tokens. Some gave holders ability to participate in the governance of a protocol; others were used to get a specific service that is hosted on blockchain. The regulators made it clear that utility tokens will only be considered utility tokens if they meet these criteria and are being sold for a platform where they can readily be utilized. Using the tokens as a fund-raising tool, however, evolves them into a security format that requires them to be regulated (Lee, 2018).

3. Security tokens

The final category is security tokens. Products that are being offered for investments are typically captured under the securities regulations. The regulators confirmed that having the ownership of an asset registered digitally on a blockchain does not alter the underlying activity, and the resulting cryptoassets are still securities from a regulatory perspective (SEC, 2019), if they meet certain prescribed tests. (*SEC.gov | Framework for "Investment Contract" Analysis of Digital Assets*, n.d.). These assets therefore will fall into the same categories that we will be familiar with in conventional financial products. Some of the key areas of securities industry that are being impacted by blockchain so far are as follows:

Crowdfunding. Raising money from the public to finance the development of a new project or company is not new. Crowdfunding has been a growing phenomenon, and the advances in FinTech have made crowdfunding platforms ever more popular. Blockchain technology can create innovations in the crowdfunding space (Cai, 2018; Lee, 2018; Chen, 2018). Blockchain is an institutional technology that replaces "trust," which required people to be organized in companies. New projects may not need to be organized as new companies and can be run in a decentralized manner, where independent contributors get rewards for their contributions. This and other innovative uses will be topic for further discussion elsewhere in this book. However, we should recognize that not having any awareness and controls during the first wave of ICOs has attracted some ill intentioned actors into this space that raised funds from the public for personal gain. It can be expected that blockchain can alter the future of crowdfunding and have some level of regulation at the same time. In fact, blockchain helps develop crowdfunding by making the implementation of regulations much simpler. For example, for many early-stage or illiquid investments, participation is open only to sophisticated or professional investors. This is to ensure that investors are knowledgeable enough to conduct due diligence on the investments and can bear the high risk and illiquidity associated with such investments. Blockchain can allow the eligibility of investors to be recorded on the blockchain and open possibilities for these investors to invest peer to peer or across a very wide platform of opportunities rather than going through a single crowdfunding platform.

Funds. Funds, particularly venture capital funds, have been the early adaptors of blockchain technology, and funds have been offered to investors in a token format. Such funds have traditionally been available only to a very limited number of investors, and blockchain technology can make it accessible to a much wider universe. There has also been an experiment of the participants of a start-up accelerator cohort to raise money collectively through a single token (22xtoken.com). Such direct access removes the hefty fees of a venture capital fund and at the same time provides the diversity that is required for a sound investment. We may therefore expect to see more such examples and models for raising funds to emerge in the future.

Listed products. Some stock exchanges around the world have been working on distributed ledger technology and are at various stages of adoption. These projects mostly entail creating the existing listed securities in a distributed ledger, which will create settlement and control efficiencies. As exchanges work with a known group of participants, they typically work with private block chain providers that can build such capabilities among the trusted participants (*FORBES | Blockchain Goes to Work*, 2019).

OTC products. Certain products such as fixed-income bonds are typically traded over the counter (OTC) between parties without a centralized exchange. There are providers that are working on improving the process for the issuance and trading of such instruments. Some of these are on private blockchains, which will be targeted toward a limited number of financial institutions, and some are testing having the tokens available on a public blockchain (Sehra et al., 2018).

Private assets. Certain assets that have historically not been in a form that could be exchanged easily may be turned into such form. This will include certain assets that were already securities legally but were very cumbersome to transfer, such as ownership interest or options of an employee on a private company. Some of them may be assets that were not available for partial ownership easily in the past and may become more easily doable in the future such as fractional ownership of art, antiques or other real-world assets. Finally, there may be assets that may come into existence that didn't exist in the past; these can be things like loyalty programs that give fans privileges, sponsorship of artists, future earnings of a sportsperson or the like. Whether such assets will be considered securities will need to be determined on a case-by-case basis, using the tests put forward by regulators looking at the format, target and intent of the transactions.

Conclusion

This chapter presented the major classifications of cryptoassets, namely cryptocurrencies, utility tokens and security tokens. It further examined the origins and key features of each category to enable the reader to compare these cryptoassets to traditional assets in a more informed way and to identify the similarities and differences. Recognizing these classifications are essential for anyone who wants to understand the risks and financial implications of these assets. While we recognize the differences among categories, we should also recognize that blockchain is a technological ecosystem, like the Internet. Therefore, these cryptoasset classes do not exist in a vacuum, and developments in one of them may have an impact on the others. For example, end-to-end processing of a security token requires them to be purchased using money, which is in a cryptocurrency format, so developments in cryptocurrencies will be an important determinant of developments in security tokens.

Overall blockchain technology can be expected to have a major impact at both the macroeconomic and the microeconomic levels. Cryptocurrencies may have important macroeconomic consequences in a wide range of areas such as unit of account for trade and investments, developments in financial surveillance and the stability of financial system. Utility tokens and platforms that are formed at the back of them can facilitate large-scale, peer-to-peer interactions, create new network effects and may allow industries and corporations to be reorganized. Adoption of security tokens can lead to change in the organization of financial markets and the roles of financial intermediaries. Digitalization of financial assets may be expected to create efficiency gains on financial products. This can have a positive impact on financial inclusion as more people can have access to financial products at a more reasonable cost. This chapter gives a glimpse into a future in which we transact in currencies that may not yet exist, on platforms where actors organize themselves in novel ways and transact in new types of financial assets. These changes, coupled with developments in the underlying technology, can alter the financial ecosystem in ways we may not yet foresee. Therefore the economic architecture of the future, built on the back of cryptoassets, will look quite different from today.

Note

1 The opinions expressed in this chapter are the author's own and do not reflect the view of their employer or any organization they are affiliated with.

References

All Cryptocurrencies | CoinMarketCap. (2020). CoinMarketCap. Retrieved March 8, 2020, from https://coinmarketcap.com/all/views/all/.

Blockchain Charts – The Total Number of Unique Blockchain.com Wallets Created. (2020). *Blockchain.com*. Retrieved June 28, 2020, from www.blockchain.com/charts/my-wallet-n-users.

Bogart, S. (2019). *Bitcoin Is a Demographic Mega-Trend: Data Analysis Medium-Blockchain Capital Blog*. Retrieved June 28, 2020, from https://medium.com/blockchain-capital-blog/bitcoin-is-a-demographic-mega-trend-data-analysis-160d2f7731e5.

Cai, C. W. (2018). Disruption of financial intermediation by FinTech : A review on crowdfunding and blockchain. *Accounting & Finance*, 58, 965–992. doi: 10.1111/acfi.12405.

Carney, M. (2018). *Mark Carney Future of Money Speech*. Retrieved from https://www.bankofengland.co.uk/-/media/boe/files/speech/2018/the-future-of-money-speech-by-mark-carney.

Carney, M. (2019). *The Growing Challenges for Monetary Policy in the Current International Monetary and Financial System*. Bank of England. Retrieved from www.bankofengland.co.uk/-/media/boe/files/speech/2019/The-growing-challenges-for-monetary-policy-speech-by-mark-carney.

Chen, Y. (2018). Blockchain tokens and the potential democratization of entrepreneurship and innovation. *Business Horizons. Kelley School of Business, Indiana University*, 61 (4), 567–575. doi: 10.1016/j.bushor.2018.03.006.

Cryptoassets Taskforce: Final Report. (2018). Retrieved from https://assets.publishing.service.gov.uk/government/uploads/system/uploads/attachment_data/file/752070/cryptoassets_taskforce_final_report_final_web.pdf.

Davidson, S., De Filippi, P., and Potts, J. (2018). Blockchains and the economic institutions of capitalism. *Journal of Instututional Economics*, 14 (4), 639–658. doi: 10.1017/S1744137417000200.

Firms That Need Authorisation | FCA. (2020). FCA. Retrieved March 8, 2020, from www.fca.org.uk/firms/authorisation/when-required.

FORBES | Blockchain Goes to Work. (2019). Retrieved July 7, 2019, from http://content.ebscohost.com/ContentServer.asp?T=P&P=AN&K=135618245&S=R&D=buh&Ebsc

oContent=dGJyMNHr7ESeprU4yOvqOLCmr1Gepq5SsKm4TK6WxWXS&Content Customer=dGJyMPGusk6vqa9MuePfgeyx44Dt6flA.

Holub, M., and Johnson, J. (2018). Bitcoin research across disciplines. *The Information Society. Taylor & Francis*, 34 (2), 114–126. doi: 10.1080/01972243.2017.1414094.

House of Commons Treasury Committee. (2018). *Crypto-Assets Twenty-Second Report of Session 2017–19 Report, Together with Formal Minutes Relating to the Report The Treasury Committee*. Retrieved from www.parliament.uk/treascom.

Lee, P. H. (2018). Crowdfunding capital in the age of blockchain-based tokens. *St. John's Law Review*, 92 (4), 833–914. Retrieved from https://heinonline.org/HOL/P?h=hein.journals/stjohn92&i=863%0Ahttps://heinonline.org/HOL/P?h=hein.journals/stjohn92&i=863.

Meaning, J., Dyson, B., Barker, J., and Clayton, E. (2018). Broadening narrow money: Monetary policy with a central bank digital currency. *SSRN*. doi: 10.2139/ssrn.3180720.

Morisse, M. (2015). Cryptocurrencies and Bitcoin: Charting the research landscape. *Proceedings of Twenty-first Americas Conference on Information Systems (AMCIS 2015)*, 1–16. doi: 10.1016/S0167-9457(01)00033-1.

Nakamoto, S. (2008). *Bitcoin: A Peer-to-Peer Electronic Cash System*. Retrieved February 21, 2020, from www.bitcoin.org.

Nelson, B. (2018). Financial stability and monetary policy issues associated with digital currencies. *Journal of Economics and Business*. doi: 10.1016/j.jeconbus.2018.06.002.

Rohr, J., and Wright, A. (2017). Blockchain-based token sales, initial coin offerings, and the democratization of public capital markets. *SSRN Electronic Journal*, 463–524. doi: 10.2139/ssrn.3048104.

SEC.gov | Framework for "Investment Contract" Analysis of Digital Assets. (n.d.). Retrieved January 22, 2020, from www.sec.gov/corpfin/framework-investment-contract-analysis-digital-assets.

Sehra, A., Cohen, R., and Arulchandran, V. (2018). *On Cryptocurrencies, Digital Assets and Private Money, Number 1 Journal of Payments Strategy & Systems*. Henry Stewart Publications. Retrieved August 24, 2019, from https://docs.wixstatic.com/ugd/5ed7cd_cc0844788d21416e99f379b1a263707f.pdf.

Sharma, Toshendra Kumar. (2019). *Security Tokens vs. Utility Tokens : A Concise Guide, Blockchain Council*. Retrieved March 8, 2019, from www.blockchain-council.org/blockchain/security-tokens-vs-utility-tokens-a-concise-guide/.

Smith, C., and Kumar, A. (2018). Crypto-currencies – an introduction to not-so-funny moneys. *Journal of Economic Surveys*, 32 (5), 1531–1559. doi: 10.1111/joes.12289.

Tschorsch, F., and Scheuermann, B. (2016). Bitcoin and beyond: A technical survey on decentralized digital currencies. *IEEE Communications Surveys and Tutorials*. doi: 10.1109/COMST.2016.2535718.

Yao, Q. (2018). A systematic framework to understand central bank digital currency. *Science China Information Sciences*. doi: 10.1007/s11432-017-9294-5.

4 The economic nature of bitcoin

Money, new gold or speculative assets?

Silvia Dal Bianco

Introduction

Bitcoin is the first cryptocurrency to be introduced. It was released in 2009 by the mysterious Satoshi Nakamoto. In its creator's words, bitcoin is "a new electronic cash system that's fully peer-to-peer, with no trusted third party" (bitcoin.org).

The aim of the present work is to understand the economic nature of bitcoin. Using the most up-to-date economic literature, this chapter clarifies whether bitcoin should be considered as money or as an asset or gold. The conclusion of the work is that bitcoin possesses the defining characteristics of a speculative asset.

The rest of the chapter is organized as follows. The second section explores whether bitcoin can be considered money. The third and fourth sections investigate the possibility that bitcoin is the "new gold" and a speculative asset, respectively. The last section concludes, portraying some policy considerations and possible lines for future research.

Is bitcoin money?

Bitcoin as a medium of exchange

Any physical or digital object that is called money carries out three economic functions: serving as medium of exchange, store of value and unit of account (Tobin, 2008). Money has also some physical desirable properties, such as, for example, durability and portability; see Lehdonvirta and Castronova (2014) for a full discussion.

Money is a medium of exchange because it is widely accepted as payment in exchange for goods and services. The role of money as an intermediary instrument allows payments to be more flexible than barter exchange (Fernandez-Villaverde, 2018).

Currently, the largest hindrance to bitcoin acting as a medium of exchange is that it is not as widely accepted as it needs to be (England & Fratrik, 2018).

According to Bundesbank Payment Statistics (2018), the amount of daily cashless transactions settled by German payment service providers alone is 200 times bigger than the daily transactions in the whole bitcoin network. Moreover, Baur et al. (2018) find that the amount of bitcoins held by users for transaction reasons has declined from 5.1 percent of total bitcoin in 2011 to 2.25 percent in 2013. Jonker (2018) observes that the low usage among consumers is matched by a low adoption by retailers. According to coinmap.org, bitcoin is accepted at 15,000 places worldwide. In comparison, there were more than 1 million payment terminals (POS) in Germany alone in 2018 (Bundesbank Payment Statistics, 2018).

The possible explanations for the low use of bitcoin as a mean of exchange are essentially two: bitcoin's price volatility and technological constraints. According to Kubát (2015), bitcoin's astounding volatility makes its purchasing power very uncertain, and this prevents its ability to act a medium of exchange. Similarly, Lo and Wang (2014) notice that returning goods is a very complicated process, as bitcoin's nominal value fluctuates a lot. For what concerns the technological constraint, Williamson (2018) observes that the potential of successful widespread adoption of bitcoin as a medium of exchange is limited by the underlying distributed ledger technology that, at the moment, cannot fully support a wider-scale payment system. Lo and Wang (2014) instead recognize that the growth of the user base in emerging economies may be constrained by the lack of digital devices, which are necessary to widely utilize bitcoin for international payments.

Despite its price volatility and possible technical implementational difficulties, bitcoin still possesses very attractive features for becoming a well accepted means of payment. According to Dourado and Brito (2014), bitcoin is superior to cash, as it can be used online, and it is more convenient than credit cards due to lower transaction fees. Moreover, as observed by Carrick (2016), bitcoins can facilitate international payments and remittances because they can be instantaneously exchanged into fiat currencies with little or no fees. As a matter of fact, up to 2013, there were no fees on transactions in bitcoin. Moreover, while the average time for traditional banking systems to complete an international payment is around five days, according to blockchain.com, the median confirmation time (i.e., the waiting time for a transaction to be accepted by the network and thus finalized) of bitcoin transaction in 2018 was only 12.9 minutes. Although, in line with Rainer et al. (2015), it must be also observed that the proof-of-work reward to miners will disappear once all bitcoins have been mined. Hence, miners might want to charge users for their efforts. Moreover, despite the fact that transaction fees are generally low, fees usually increase when the bitcoin trade volume increases, such as in December 2017 when the average transaction fee reached USD 55.16 (BitInfoCharts, 2019).

In conclusion, bitcoin is currently far from being universally accepted as a medium of exchange.

Bitcoin as a store of value

The second economic property of money is acting as a store of value. To this end, a currency must be able to sustain a stable level of worth for a prolonged period of time (Tobin, 2008).

Ammous (2018) argues that bitcoin has the potential to serve as a store of value. This is due to the system design and, in particular, to the credible commitment to the predetermined pace of bitcoin supply that is fully embedded in its protocol, as well as by the absence of any authority capable of altering the bitcoin supply schedule. Both features should prevent sudden changes in purchasing power. However, Williamson (2018) criticizes the system's design by arguing that, although there is a fixed mining schedule, bitcoin does not have a guaranteed low growth rate because the whole system could be potentially replicated, as the software is open source. Moreover, according to De la Horra et al. (2019), the lack of a central bank to control price volatility and thus the intrinsic impossibility of monetary stabilization policies might expose the system to huge instability.

Hayes (2019) supports the idea that bitcoin can serve as a store of value because its price, although volatile, can be predicted using the marginal cost of production model. Based on ordinary least squares (OLS) regression, 81 percent of the observed market prices, taken in five-year averages, between June 2013 and April 2019 can be explained by the marginal cost of mining, which, similarly to Fantazzini (2018), depends on electricity costs and computational power. Such a result signals that the purchasing power of bitcoin is predictable.

The predictability of bitcoin purchasing power is put under close scrutiny by a series of works. Rainer et al. (2015) analyze the USD/bitcoin exchange rate, showing that there have been sharp movements between 2013 and 2015 and thus that the value of bitcoin is far from being stable. Further empirical evidence on this point is offered by Klein et al. (2018). Using a BEKK-GARCH model, the authors estimate time-varying conditional correlations between bitcoin prices and the S&P 500. They find that bitcoin value is too volatile and hence not stable over time. A similar view is portrayed by Corbet et al. (2018). They conclude that future contracts have not provided more stability or predictability to bitcoin value.

In conclusion, the majority of the most up-to date literature seems to agree on the fact that bitcoin does not act as a store of value.

Bitcoin as a unit of account

A unit of account assigns a value to goods and services using a common specific currency, allowing the price of goods to be compared easily (Tobin, 2008). England and Fratrik (2018) note that bitcoin serves as a unit of account between itself and other altcoins, but it does not act as a numeraire for the majority of goods and services. Actually, Lo and Wang (2014) suggest that the unit of account function is related to the medium of exchange one, as it requires merchants to display prices in bitcoin. However, the huge volatility of bitcoin's price acts as a major source of confusion for consumers, and it can generate menu costs for merchants. Dourado and Brito (2014) consider the possibility of denominating the transactions in dollars but settling them in bitcoins. Hence, bitcoin could serve as a medium of exchange without being a unit of account. Interestingly, England and Fratrik (2018) provide supporting anecdotal evidence, showing that prices are usually converted to bitcoin at the last stage of the sale.

In conclusion, bitcoin does not serve as a unit of account.

Is bitcoin the new gold?

Bitcoin and gold share some interesting features (see England and Fratrik (2018), Ammous (2018) and Klein et al. (2018) for details). In particular, both bitcoin and gold are in limited supply, they require an energy-intense mining process to come to light, they are both durable as well as divisible and they cannot be easily counterfeited (in the case of gold this is due to its chemical stability; in the case of bitcoin this is due to the proof of work). However, only gold can act both as a hedge and as a safe haven. An asset can be described as a hedge if, on average, it is negatively correlated with another asset; while it can be further classified as a safe haven if it acts as a hedge during times of stress. Employing daily data on bitcoin and the commodity indices from July 18, 2010, to December 28, 2015, Bouri et al. (2017) confirm bitcoin hedge function but not the one of safe haven. Similarly, Stensas et al. (2019) find that bitcoin serves as a hedge for investors in most of the developing countries such as Brazil, Russia, India and South Korea but not as a safe haven. Hence, bitcoin is not new gold.

Bitcoin as a speculative asset

The present work has shown that, at present, bitcoin cannot be considered money or as new gold. At this point, it is interesting to question whether it can be considered an asset. A resource is considered an asset if it is owned or controlled with the expectation that it will provide a future benefit (IASB, 2015). More technically, the fundamental value of an asset is represented by the expected present value of the stream of future dividends attached to the asset (Iraola & Santos, 2008). Then the fundamental theorem of asset pricing (see Dybvig & Ross, 1987) guarantees that the equilibrium market price of any asset equals its fundamental value. When trading in assets occurs at a higher price than its fundamental value, this is called speculative behavior (Harrison and Kreps, 1978).

De la Horra et al. (2019) argue that bitcoin has no fundamental value because it does not generate any income streams. This observation is in line with the so-called Keynesian beauty contest (Keynes, 1936, p. 156). According to this, market prices depend not on the fundamental value of an asset but rather on what investors think their value is. Hence, the sentiment, or investors' beliefs, drives the value of a financial asset. The Keynesian beauty contest hypothesis has received empirical confirmation. For example, the original work of Kristoufek (2013) shows that there is a strong statistically significant correlation between the bitcoin prices and the daily Wikipedia searches and weekly Google Trends, which proxy for media attention. Karalevicious (2017) uses psychosemantic dictionaries, namely the *Harvard Psychosocial Dictionary* and Loughran-McDonald finance-specific dictionary, to show that bitcoin trading does not occur on fundamentals but rather on investors' sentiment. Bouoiyour and Selmi (2017) find that the attractiveness of bitcoin from investors' perspective, which is proxied by daily views from Google Trends, has a short-run positive impact on the cryptocurrency price dynamics.

For what concerns the speculative nature of bitcoin as an asset, Rainer et al. (2015) show that the majority of users buy and store bitcoin in their wallets but subsequently hold on to the purchased bitcoin instead of spending it on other goods or services. This evidence is complemented by Baur et al. (2018) showing that, in 2013, 34.13 percent of bitcoins were held by investors. Further, Lo and Wang (2014) document that the transaction/exchange ratio has been quite low between 2011 and 2014. This indicator represents the ratio between the transaction volume (i.e., the number of transactions processed across the bitcoin network) and the exchange volume (i.e., the number of bitcoin traded on exchanges against fiat currencies). Hence, this evidence indicates the low popularity of bitcoin as a medium of exchange. More recently, De la Horra et al. (2019) calculates that the daily transaction/exchange ratio averaged to 0.29 in 2017. The estimated value suggest that only 30 percent of bitcoin daily transactions are for the purpose of trade, and the remaining 70 percent are possibly for speculation. Finally, for what concerns speculative bubbles, Fantazzini (2018) employs the explosive bubble framework developed by Evans (1991) and finds numerous price bubbles especially in the 2013–2014 period. Fernandez-Villaverde (2018) reaches the same conclusion, assuming that bitcoin is a pure fiat private currency, so that any value assigned to it is a bubble by definition. Recently, Hayes (2019) suggests the existence of bitcoin price bubbles, when bitcoin prices deviate from the bitcoin marginal cost of production.

Conclusion

This work has employed the most up-to-date economic literature to investigate the economic nature of bitcoin. The conclusion reached is threefold. First, at present, bitcoin does not absolve the three key economic functions of money, hence it is not money. Second, bitcoin cannot be classified as a safe haven; hence it is not the new gold. Third, consistently with the Keynesian beauty context hypothesis, bitcoin's fundamental value is related to investors' beliefs on the stream of future earnings. Further, its price trend seems to have been often characterized by price bubbles. Hence, the economic nature of bitcoin is the one of a speculative asset.

From the policy perspective, it does not seem that bitcoin might undermine the stability of the financial system, as their diffusion and usage are quite limited. However, the idea of an Internet native currency is extremely attractive, especially because it could allow transferring value at zero transaction costs.

The cryptocurrency launched by Facebook in 2019, the Libra coin, represents a very interesting development. It features decentralization as well as vital endorsements and financial backing from reputable global companies. It has caught the eye of many institutions, including the Bank of England. In particular, regulators around the world are worried on the one hand that, thanks to Facebook's global reach, Libra could compete with the USD and, on the other, that the stability of the global financial system could be undermined, as Facebook's blueprint fails to address risks around financial security, investor protection and anti–money laundering laws.

More research on bitcoin as a payment system is needed to assess whether an Internet native digital currency could be effectively and credibly implemented.

References

Ammous, S. (2018). Can cryptocurrencies fulfil the functions of money? *The Quarterly Review of Economics and Finance*, 70, 38–51.

Baur, D. G., Hong, K., and Lee, A. D. (2018). Bitcoin: Medium of exchange or speculative assets? *Journal of International Financial Markets, Institutions and Money, Elsevier*, 54(C), 177–189.

BitInfoCharts. (2019). *Bitcoin (BTC) Price Stats and Information*. Online Edition. Retrieved August 24, 2020, from https://bitinfocharts.com/bitcoin/.

Bouoiyour, J., and Selmi, R. (2017). *The Bitcoin Price Formation: Beyond the Fundamental Sources*. Retrieved from https://arxiv.org/pdf/1707.01284.pdf.

Bouri, E., Jalkh, N., Molnar, P., and Roubaud, D. (2017). Bitcoin for energy commodities before and after the December 2013 crash: Diversifier, hedge or safe haven? *Applied Economics*, 49 (49–51), October–November, 5063–5073.

Bundesbank Payment Statistics. (2018). Retrieved from www.bundesbank.de/en/service/reporting-systems/banking-statistics/payments-statistics-620072.

Carrick, J. (2016). Bitcoin as a complement to emerging market currencies. *Emerging Markets Finance and Trade*, 52 (10), 2321–2334.

Corbet, S., Lucey, B., Peat, M., and Vigne, S. (2018). Bitcoin futures – what use are they? *Economics Letters, Elsevier*, 172(C), 23–27.

De la Horra, L. P., de la Fuente, G., and Perote, J. (2019). The drivers of Bitcoin demand: A short and long-run analysis. *International Review of Financial Analysis*, 62, March, 21–34.

Dourado, E., and Brito, J. (2014). Cryptocurrency. In Steven N. Durlauf and Lawrence E. Blume (eds.), *The New Palgrave Dictionary of Economics*. Online Edition. Retrieved from https://www.mercatus.org/system/files/cryptocurrency-article.pdf.

Dybvig, P. H., and Ross, S. A. (1987). Arbitrage. In J. Eatwell, M. Milgate, and P. Newman (eds.), *The New Palgrave: A Dictionary of Economics* (Vol. 1). London: Palgrave Macmillan.

England, C., and Fratrik, C. (2018). Where to Bitcoin? *Journal of Private Enterprise, Spring*, 33 (1), 9–30.

Evans, G. W. (1991). Pitfalls in testing for explosive bubbles in asset prices. *The American Economic Review*, 81 (4), September, 922–930.

Fantazzini, D. (2018). *Bitcoin Econometrics*. Presented at Moscow School of Economics, Moscow.

Fernandez-Villaverde, J. (2018). *Cryptocurrencies: A Crash Course in Digital Monetary Economics*. Penn Institute for Economic Research, Department of Economics, University of Pennsylvania, PIER Working Paper Archive.

Harrison, M., and Kreps, D. (1978). Speculative investor behavior in a stock market with heterogeneous expectations. *Quarterly Journal of Economics*, XCII, 323–336.

Hayes, A. S. (2019). Bitcoin price and its marginal cost of production: Support for a fundamental value. *Applied Economics Letters*, 26 (7), April, 554–560.

IASB (International Accounting Standards Board). (2015). *FRS for SMEs*. London. p. 15. ISBN: 978-0-409-04813-1.

Iraola, M. A., and Santos, M. S. (2008). Speculative bubbles. In Palgrave Macmillan (eds.), *The New Palgrave Dictionary of Economics*. London: Palgrave Macmillan.

Jonker, N. (2018). *What Drives Bitcoin Adoption by Retailers Netherlands Central Bank*. Research Department, DNB Working Papers.

Karalevicious, V. (2017). Using sentiment analysis to predict interday Bitcoin price movements. *Journal of Risk Finance*, 19 (1), 56–75.

Keynes, J. M. (1936). *The General Theory of Employment, Interest and Money*. New York: Harcourt Brace and Co.

Klein, T., Hien, P., and Walther, T. (2018). Bitcoin is not the new gold: A comparison of volatility, correlation, and portfolio performance. *International Review of Financial Analysis*, 59, 105–116.

Kristoufek, L. (2013). Bitcoin meets google trends and Wikipedia: Quantifying the relationship between phenomena of the Internet era. *Scientific Reports*, 3, 116.

Kubát, M. (2015). Virtual currency Bitcoin in the scope of money definition and store of value. *Procedia Economics and Finance*, 30, 409–416.

Lehdonvirta, V., and Castronova, E. (2014). Money. In *Virtual Economies: Design and Analysis* (pp. 177–196). Cambridge, MA: The MIT Press.

Lo, S., and Wang, J. C. (2014). *Bitcoin as Money? Federal Reserve Bank of Boston*. Current Policy Perspectives No 14–4.

Rainer, B., Christin, N., Edelman, F., and Moore, T. (2015). Bitcoin: Economics, technology, and governance. *Journal of Economic Perspectives*, 29 (2), 213–238.

Stensås, A., Nygaard, M. F., Kyaw, K., and Treepongkaruna, S. (2019). Can Bitcoin be a diversifier, hedge or safe haven tool? *Cogent Economics & Finance*, 8 (1).

Tobin, J. (2008). Money. In Palgrave Macmillan (eds.), *The New Palgrave Dictionary of Economics*. London: Palgrave Macmillan.

Williamson, S. (2018). Is Bitcoin a waste of resources? Federal Reserve Bank of St. Louis review. *Second Quarter*, 100 (2), 107–115.

5 The microeconomics of cryptocurrencies

Guych Nuryyev, David W. Savitski and John E. Peterson

Introduction

Bitcoin was the first and largest cryptocurrency, with market capitalization exceeding USD 209 billion, representing 67.3 percent of the total cryptocurrency market capitalization.[1] Given its success, thousands of cryptocurrencies have subsequently emerged.[2]

The initial surge consisted of initial coin offerings (ICOs). An ICO accepts fiat money or bitcoins in exchange for the new cryptocurrency. Later, initial exchange offerings (IEOs) emerged. An IEO is a variant of an ICO that is listed on a platform of an existing cryptocurrency exchange. In 2017 and 2018, cryptocurrency sales raised USD 6.5 and USD 21.6 billion,[3] pushing market capitalization of the cryptocurrencies listed on CoinMarketCap to USD 835.5 billion in January 2018. Most of these cryptocurrencies were created to cash in on the hype, and many have lost at least 95 percent of their peak value. While their aggregate value has fallen, the USD 300 billion market capitalization makes cryptocurrencies relevant.

To examine its relevance, we focus on how bitcoin performs the functions of money. Other cryptocurrencies are discussed when relevant for a particular monetary topic. A better understanding of where cryptocurrencies fall short of fiat money might allow for a better design and might possibly decrease price volatility.

Medium of exchange

General acceptance

The medium of exchange function means a generally accepted form of payment. The Haitian gourde (HTG), for example, is fiat money in Haiti. It is difficult, however, to make purchases in Norway with HTG. Hence, general acceptance of various forms of fiat money is limited.

Globally, bitcoin is accepted by individuals and firms. The average weekly (annual) transaction volume[4] equals the annual GDP of Haiti (Norway). Bitcoin is not, however, generally accepted everywhere. This limits bitcoin's medium of exchange function to mostly online transactions. Bitcoin's acceptance function is independent of its unit of account function: a sender would transfer an amount of bitcoin equal to the desired dollar value.

Transaction cost

To function as a medium of exchange, a currency needs a low transaction cost. Transaction costs have both domestic and international dimensions. International wire transfers are expensive fiat money transactions. The typical international wire transfer fee is USD 60 (Tierney, 2019). For a wire transfer of USD 2,000, the fee is 3 percent. International wire transfers also typically take several business days. Fiat money transaction fees also vary widely within national borders. The typical domestic wire transfer fee is USD 40 (Tierney, 2019). While exchanging cash hand-to-hand has no transaction fee, it only works locally.

Bitcoin transactions, alternatively, are not constrained by national borders and happen within minutes or hours, depending on sender fees. The historical average fee is 0.091 percent.[5] The largest transaction took place on May 29, 2019,[6] was valued at almost USD 1.4 billion and had a USD 106.50 transaction fee.

The most expensive cryptocurrency transaction involves converting into and out of fiat money. Coinbase (the U.S.-based cryptocurrency exchange) charges 0.4 percent for converting between bitcoin and USD (Khatri, 2019). BitoEx (Taiwan's cryptocurrency exchange) doesn't charge a fee but has a price spread of around 4 percent.[7] Hence, the cost of converting into and out of fiat money varies significantly across countries.

As noted, cryptocurrency is faster and sometimes cheaper for international and long-distance domestic transactions, whereas fiat money is cheaper for local domestic transactions. Hence, cryptocurrency could potentially make international money transfers faster and cheaper. Converting into and out of fiat money, however, increases the cost.

Transaction costs and technology

The Lightning Network technology reduces transaction costs for parties that can pool bitcoin transactions without converting into and out of fiat currency each time. Lightning Network parties can transact multiple times, decreasing transaction costs by orders of magnitude. Transaction costs are approximately 0.0005 percent to 0.005 percent (BitMEX Research, 2019). Lightning Network parties can also pay anyone else within the network using jumps through several connections. These transactions create a multisignature address with time lock capability, eliminating the need to trust counterparties.

For example, Alan wants to pay Cathy, but he only has a connection with Bob, who has a connection with Cathy. To pay Cathy, Alan pays Bob and arranges Bob's automatic payment to Cathy of the same amount, where Bob collects a negligible fee.

There are, however, disadvantages of the Lightning Network. Closing the tap (say, to send the balance to an exchange and convert into fiat money) requires two blockchain transactions at a fee. Currently, this is not a popular payment method, however; the amount locked in the network during June–October 2019 fluctuated between USD 6 and USD 12 million,[8] about 1 percent of bitcoin's average daily volume.

Unit of account

Unit of account and general acceptance

The unit of account function is a measurement function. Widespread acceptance and stability are necessary for a currency to effectively perform this function. The USD and euro are two popular examples.

Sometimes a foreign currency functions as a unit of account for particular transactions. Often it is used as forex reserves (USD, euro, etc.) that function as a unit of account in foreign countries. For example, in the mid-1990s, during the high inflation in post-Soviet countries, the USD often functioned as a unit of account for transactions involving valuable assets (cars, apartments, etc.).

Given price volatility and limited acceptance, bitcoin is unlikely to become a unit of account for offline transactions. An alternate cryptocurrency that could serve as a unit of account is a stablecoin, which is pegged to an asset or group of assets, mitigating price volatility. For example, Tether is pegged to the USD through the fiat reserves held by Tether Ltd.[9] Considerable counterparty risks exist, however, with centralized cryptocurrencies. If Tether Ltd. were to mismanage their reserves, for example, owners of tether coins are likely to suffer substantial losses.

Examples of foreign units of account

Fiat currencies have long performed the unit of account function in foreign countries: for example, post-Soviet countries in the mid-1990s and Zimbabwe in the mid- to late 2000s. Stable fiat currencies, such as the USD and euro, have also existed longer than cryptocurrencies. Yet there is growing evidence of cryptocurrency's increasing use as a foreign unit of account.

Venezuela has somewhat widespread acceptance of bitcoin payments (Gholam, 2018) due to its hyperinflation, which reached almost 1.7 million percent in 2018 (Callama, 2019). In such an environment, many Venezuelans use bitcoin for transactions and store of value (Meredith, 2019). Weekly transaction volume on a popular P2P (peer-to-peer) exchange (LocalBitcoins) reached the second highest level in the world after Russia (Hernandez, 2019). Converting bitcoins into bolivars is costly, however, as bank transfers exceeding USD 50 in bolivars are frozen for investigation. Hence, many high-end businesses (jewelers, restaurants, doctors, travel agents, etc.) started accepting bitcoin payments, whereas few basic and staple goods sellers accept bitcoins (Cuen, 2019; Sourus, 2019).

Venezuela is the first hyperinflationary event that has taken place since the creation of bitcoin and shows that a relatively widespread acceptance of bitcoin payments is achievable when the local currency suffers from hyperinflation. Also, with high inflation and government mistrust, numerous African countries are growing bitcoin hotspots.

Store of value

The store of value function means that money can be saved with relatively predictable future value. Other assets used as a store of value include art, gold and wine. These assets are favored as a store of value because of their rarity and hence low risk of devaluation. Currently in developed countries, bitcoin appears to be used more as a speculative asset (like art and wine) rather than as a low-risk store of value (like gold).

Volatility

High price volatility makes the future value of bitcoin unpredictable, diminishing its ability to store value. Daily price volatility against the USD was 3.7 percent during January–November 2019.[10] If bitcoin's market capitalization growth in recent years continues,[11] however, it might reduce price volatility. Greater market capitalization requires greater capital flow to change the price by the same percentage. For example, compare price volatility of gold in the first ten years after President Richard Nixon abolished the gold standard to that of the most recent ten years: during September 1971–August 1981, weekly price volatility was 3.93 percent, nearly double that during December 2009–November 2019, when it was 2.04 percent.[12]

A stablecoin has lower price volatility than bitcoin. Daily price volatility of tether was 0.28 percent during January–November 2019.[13] Using stablecoin as a store of value appears redundant, however, as one can use the underlying fiat money.

The value of fiat money also changes versus goods and services (inflation). Relative stability of fiat money is the goal of many central banks. Annualized inflation for major fiat currencies[14] during January–October 2019 was 1.74 percent in the United States, 1.24 percent in the European Union, and 2.58 percent in China. Such price stability discourages the use of bitcoin. In contrast, many African countries have high and prolonged inflation. Furthermore, a significant portion of the population lacks access to traditional banking. Both of these factors have encouraged bitcoin usage there.

Rarity

As noted, rarity encourages using bitcoin as a store of value. The total supply of bitcoin is limited to 21 million bitcoins, to be reached approximately in 2140. Currently, supply increases by approximately 1,800 bitcoins per day, about 3.6 percent annual growth of the current supply of 18 million bitcoins. This growth halves approximately every four years.

Undermining the limited supply of bitcoin is the fact that there are many alternate coins. Hence, while a supply limit applies to bitcoin, the aggregate supply is unlimited. In the long run, however, many newly created cryptocurrencies are likely to become negligible. Two factors are likely to drive this elimination process.

First, only decentralized cryptocurrencies might function as a store of value based on rarity. A cryptocurrency that is not decentralized is not free of counterparty risk; it cannot function as a store of value in the long run, as there is risk of unlimited inflation as with fiat currency. After the cryptocurrency hype of 2017, at least 1,818 cryptocurrencies have disappeared for similar reasons.[15] This parallels the many Internet-related businesses appearing during and disappearing shortly after the dot-com bubble.

Second, there is a first-mover advantage in acquiring general adoption of a decentralized cryptocurrency. The network effect might lead to the concentration of adoption of very few decentralized cryptocurrencies with limited supply. Bitcoin's dominance of total cryptocurrency market capitalization illustrates this. This dominance has doubled since the all-time low of 32.8 percent in January 2018, the peak of the cryptocurrency hype.

Technological dimension

Financial privacy

Bitcoin provides users with other valuable features, such as financial privacy. Fiat money in the form of physical cash offers excellent privacy. Location and transaction size, however, can limit cash payments. Cash payments over a given size are sometimes difficult: India's overnight ban of high-denomination notes on November 8, 2016, failed to reduce illegal activity significantly (Reserve Bank of India, 2016; Beniwal, 2018); the Australian government is considering a ban on cash purchases over USD 10,000 AUD (Khadem, 2019). In addition, financial privacy is gradually eroding with the proliferation of electronic payments, e.g., PayPal, Mastercard, Visa and WeChat Pay. A related issue is financial censorship, which becomes possible without financial privacy.

Bitcoin allows users to maintain financial privacy and prevent financial censorship, which might be important in certain cases, e.g., for whistleblowers. In 2010, Visa, Mastercard and PayPal banned donations to WikiLeaks (Addley & Halliday, 2010). This ban was possible due to lack of financial privacy: payment processors are aware of the identities of senders and receivers of money. After the ban, donations to WikiLeaks were made in bitcoin.

While bitcoin provides some financial privacy and protection from censorship, its blockchain data is public. Modern analytical tools allow searching for address associations, possibly revealing identities if at least one of the associated addresses has been connected with a cryptocurrency exchange complying with know your customer (KYC) regulations.

There are privacy-oriented cryptocurrencies that prevent such analysis. Monero (13th largest cryptocurrency as of August 5, 2019) is the largest privacy-oriented cryptocurrency. Similar to bitcoin, mining creates monero, and it is decentralized. Monero improves financial privacy with cryptography. Ring signatures (where several senders jointly sign transactions to several receivers) make it difficult to identify a particular sender(s)–receiver(s) combination. Stealth addresses make this identification more difficult by generating a one-time temporary address for every transaction.

Money laundering

Money laundering is often raised regarding the financial privacy provided by cryptocurrencies. U.S. President Barack Obama emphasized this issue in one of his speeches (Carson, 2016). Due to difficulty of tracing cryptocurrency payments, they are sometimes used for illegal activities, including money laundering. Over 65,000 listings at 18 dark net markets were reported in 2014 (Digital Citizens Alliance, 2014). Privacy-oriented cryptocurrencies, such as monero, are becoming more widespread in dark net markets compared to bitcoin (Redman, 2016; Thompson, 2018). To combat this, governments introduce KYC and anti–money laundering (AML) regulations for cryptocurrency exchanges.

The use of fiat money in money laundering is also a serious problem. In 2017, in the United States alone, money laundering was estimated at USD 200 billion (Finextra Research, 2017). Extrapolating this amount to the global level would dwarf the market capitalization of all cryptocurrencies combined.

Security

Millions of dollars have been hacked from crypto exchanges,[16] encouraging owners to hold cryptocurrency on their devices rather than on exchanges. Personal devices, however, might also be hacked or lost. Therefore, computer security is a major concern with cryptocurrency.

The cost of securing individual devices, however, reduces counterparty risk. In contrast, banks might mismanage fiat money, although many countries have deposit insurance. Bank losses might lead to haircuts on larger deposits.[17] Additionally, bitcoin (similar to art or wine) is free from having its supply inflated.

Bitcoin security also relates to owners' ability to prevent confiscation. Securing bitcoin can be boiled down to memorizing a string of words. Even if a confiscating body is aware that an individual owns bitcoins, bitcoin security allows for plausible deniability: memorizing different words for different addresses and providing the pass phrase with lower funds under duress. This is useful in countries with corrupt law enforcement. On the international scale, bitcoin is easier to secure than fiat currency, or art, or gold, etc. Russia's money held in foreign bank accounts, for example, can be frozen by foreign entities.

Conclusions

Fiat currencies are the dominant forms of currency today. Yet with the coming of the digital age, cryptocurrencies are emerging as competitors. Their success depends on their ability to mimic fiat currency. Perhaps the greatest disadvantage concerns volatility. They have several offsetting advantages, however, from supply limits to privacy. How well they emerge as competitors depends on how the dominant fiat currencies perform in the future.

Notes

1 Cryptocurrencies listed on CoinMarketCap (on https://coinmarketcap.com) as of August 5, 2019. All amounts are in U.S. dollars.
2 There were 2,302 cryptocurrencies listed on CoinMarketCap as of August 5, 2019.
3 www.coinschedule.com/stats.
4 Average daily transaction volume during November 9, 2017–November 9, 2019 was USD 1,188 million (www.blockchain.com/en/charts/estimated-transaction-volume-usd?timespan=2years).
5 Average transaction fee during November 9, 2017–November 9, 2019 (www.blockchain.com/charts/transaction-fees?timespan=2years).
6 Blockchain (blockchain explorer and search engine) (https://blockchair.com/bitcoin/transactions?s=output_total_usd(desc)#).
7 Bitcoin price spread at BitoEx.com (www.bitoex.com/charts?locale=en).
8 Defi Pulse, Lightning Network (https://defipulse.com/lightning-network).
9 Tether (seventh largest cryptocurrency as of August 5, 2019) is the largest stablecoin by market capitalization (https://tether.to).
10 Standard deviation based on data from Investing.com (www.investing.com/crypto/bitcoin/btc-usd-historical-data).
11 Annually, bitcoin's market capitalization dropped in two years in the last decade: in 2014 and 2018.
12 Calculated as standard deviation based on data from Investing.com (www.investing.com/currencies/xau-usd-historical-data).
13 Standard deviation based on data from Investing.com (www.investing.com/crypto/tether/usdt-usd-historical-data).
14 Trading Economics (https://tradingeconomics.com/country-list/inflation-rate).
15 Dead Coins, Full List (https://deadcoins.com).
16 During January–June 2019, USD 70 million was stolen in six hacks of cryptocurrency exchanges (www.saturn.network/blog/cryptopia-exchange-hacked-again/;
    https://twitter.com/Cryptopia_NZ/status/1085084168852291586;
    www.coindesk.com/crypto-exchange-bithumb-hacked-for-13-million-in-suspected-insider-job;
    https://techcrunch.com/2019/05/10/binance-security-hack/;
    www.theblockcrypto.com/linked/26370/hackers-stole-as-much-as-10m-in-ripple-in-a-gatehub-hack;
    https://cointelegraph.com/news/singaporean-exchange-bitrue-gets-hacked-losing-5-million-in-xrp-cardano).
17 Wikipedia, 2012–2013 Cypriot financial crisis (https://en.wikipedia.org/wiki/2012%E2%80%9313_Cypriot_financial_crisis).

References

Addley, E., and Halliday, J. (2010). Operation payback cripples MasterCard site in revenge for WikiLeaks ban. *The Guardian*. Retrieved from www.theguardian.com/media/2010/dec/08/operation-payback-mastercard-website-wikileaks.

Beniwal, V. (2018). Few hits and many misses from India's cash ban after 2 years. *Bloomberg*. Retrieved from www.bloomberg.com/news/articles/2018-09-23/few-hits-and-many-misses-from-india-s-cash-ban-after-two-years.

BitMEX Research. (2019). The lightning network (Part 2) – routing fee economics. *BitMEX*. Retrieved from https://blog.bitmex.com/the-lightning-network-part-2-routing-fee-economics.

Callama, B. (2019). Asamblea Nacional: inflacion de 2018 cerro en 1 698 488 %. *El Universal*, January 9. Retrieved from www.eluniversal.com/economia/30108/la-inflacion-de-diciembre-fue-1418-abriendo-2019-en-1698488.

Carson, B. (2016). OBAMA: If government can't access phones, 'everybody is walking around with a Swiss Bank account in their pocket.' *Business Insider*. Retrieved from www.businessinsider.com/obama-comments-on-encryption-at-sxsw-2016-3.

Cuen, L. (2019). What's holding back Bitcoin in Venezuela? This group is investigating. *Coindesk*. Retrieved from www.coindesk.com/whats-holding-back-bitcoin-in-venezuela-this-group-is-investigating.

Digital Citizens Alliance. (2014). Dark net. August. Retrieved from www.digitalcitizensalliance.org/get-informed/darknet-august-2014.

Finextra Research. (2017). *Online Payments – The Blind Spot in the ALM Regime*. Retrieved from www.finextra.com/blogposting/14298/online-payments-the-blind-spot-in-the-aml-regime.

Gholam, H. R. P. (2018). In Venezuela, Bitcoin is a lifeline. *Long Hash*, July 10. Retrieved from www.longhash.com/news/in-venezuela-bitcoin-is-a-lifeline.

Hernandez, C. (2019). Bitcoin has saved my family. *The New York Times*, February 23. Retrieved from www.nytimes.com/2019/02/23/opinion/sunday/venezuela-bitcoin-inflation-cryptocurrencies.html.

Khadem, N. (2019). Cash-ban law under review as MPs argue it would push people into "clutches of the banks," restrict freedom. *ABC*. Retrieved from www.abc.net.au/news/2019-10-25/cash-ban-law-under-inqury-post-mp-concerns-on-freedom-breach/11640124.

Khatri, Y. (2019). Coinbase pro has good and bad news regarding fees for traders. *Coindesk*. Retrieved from www.co.indesk.com/coinbase-pro-has-good-and-bad-news-regarding-fees-for-traders.

Meredith, S. (2019). Bitcoin trading in crisis-stricken Venezuela has just hit an all-time high. *CNBC*, February 14. Retrieved from www.cnbc.com/2019/02/14/venezuela-crisis-bitcoin-trading-volumes-hit-an-all-time-high-.html.

Redman, J. (2016). Leading dark net markets to support Monero. *Bitcoin.com*. Retrieved from https://news.bitcoin.com/leading-dark-net-markets-support-monero.

Reserve Bank of India. (2016). *Withdrawal of Legal Tender Status for ₹ 500 and ₹ 1000 Notes: RBI Notice*. Retrieved from www.rbi.org.in/Scripts/BS_PressReleaseDisplay.aspx?prid=38520.

Sourus, K. (2019). Bitcoin in Venezuela. *Fifi Finance*. Retrieved from https://fififinance.com/venezuela/bitcoin.

Thompson, P. (2018). Is dark net done with Bitcoin? *CoinTelegraph*. Retrieved from https://cointelegraph.com/news/is-darknet-done-with-bitcoin.

Tierney, S. (2019). Wire transfers: What banks charge. *NerdWallet*. Retrieved from www.nerdwallet.com/blog/banking/wire-transfers-what-banks-charge/.

Part II

Cryptocurrencies in industry

6 The sources of cybersecurity threats in cryptocurrency

Valtteri Kaartemo and Marius Kramer

Cryptocurrencies and the blockchain technology behind them have been hailed for overcoming many of the challenges of fiat money. While people interested in cryptocurrencies have also heard about potential security threats, they are relatively little known by average cryptocurrency users. However, they are important, as cybersecurity attacks on cryptocurrencies can significantly influence the use and value of any cryptocurrency. Various criminal activities cause the loss of over USD 1 billion annually (Europol, 2019). And even if a fork might save the system, attacks can have a long-term impact on the future of a cryptocurrency.

The purpose of this chapter is to increase the understanding on the sources of cybersecurity threats in cryptocurrency. We review the extant literature to identify the most common sources of cybersecurity threats in cryptocurrency literature, more specifically those of 51 percent attacks, sybil attacks, eclipse attacks and spam attacks, as well as introduce one attack that is not discussed in the academic literature, namely GitHub attacks. In addition to reviewing the literature, we provide illustrative examples of the attacks and methods to prevent the attacks. We also contribute by suggesting future research avenues to improve cybersecurity in cryptocurrency. Due to space limitations, we are not able to discuss all cybersecurity threats in cryptocurrency. For the readers interested in wider reviews, we recommend referring to reviews of blockchain security in general (Li et al., 2017; Saad et al., 2019; Zhu et al., 2018), security and adversarial strategies of proof-of-work (PoW) cryptocurrencies (Gervais et al., 2016) or vulnerabilities of smart contracts (Atzei et al., 2017; Chen et al., 2019).

51% attacks

In 51% attacks, a hostile node gets a majority of voting power and can introduce changes to the blockchain. This enables, for instance, double spending of coins, when the node in power can alter the transaction history. This requires people to trust that the actor behind 51 percent of hashing power has good intents.

For PoW coins, there are basically three ways to get into the majority position. First, one can buy enough equipment to get the majority of hashing power. For bitcoin, the hardware cost is estimated around USD 20 billion (*Cost of a 51% Attack*, 2020). While this might be too much for a criminal attempt, it is also possible to rent enough hashing power. *Crypto 51* (2020) shows how much it theoretically costs to run a one-hour attack against a cryptocurrency. The price varies from less than USD 1 (Euno, Straks, Halcyon) to close to USD 1 million (bitcoin) as of early 2020.

Second, a majority position might result from the willingness of cryptocurrency miners to join their forces. Due to high difficulty, solo miners (those not partaking in a mining pool or building a mining farm) of PoW cryptocurrencies would take hundreds of years on average to solve a block even with the latest specialized equipment. Therefore, the miners tend to join the mining pool with the highest hash power. In these pools, the profits from mining are shared with the miners. While these pools are in general useful for individual miners, they can be a cybersecurity threat for the system, as pool operators can perform certain attacks on the network as soon as their pool reaches a majority of the voting power (Bastiaan, 2015). With 51 percent of voting power, miners are able to make changes to the original blockchain and double-spend the coins. This centralization of PoW coins is dangerous for their security. For instance, bitcoin is extremely centralized and has faced a situation in which Bitmain had a majority of the voting power. The only factor currently still protecting bitcoin is a social one.

Third, it is possible for one malicious intern of a pool with minimal skills to take over a large pool with 51 percent for a short amount of time and launch a double-spend attack. Therefore, it is not enough that we rely on a good faith of these mining pools. A 51% attack could be initiated through social engineering, blackmail, coercion or hacking. Given that you could take over a cryptocurrency worth billions of dollars, the criminals might be willing to spend several millions to do so. While we do not know how many times this has been attempted, this is a serious concern that would have a serious impact on bitcoin, which would be forked to BTC classic and BTC, and in the case of bitcoin, this would have a tremendous impact on the whole cryptocurrency market.

The threat of 51% attack can be fixed with new hybrids that combine PoW with PoS (VeriCoin & Verium, Decred, Ethereum's Casper). There can also be side-chain scaling that prevents 51% attacks (Cardano, Skycoin, Elastos, Lisk, Ark, Ardor), or more voting power can be given to trustworthy nodes (IOST's Proof-of-Believability). Finally, PoW-only coins can introduce new rules that restrict the size of large mining pools to 5 percent of the entire hash rate.

Sybil attacks

Sybil attacks are considered to be the most challenging threat for security in permissionless architectures (Otte et al., 2017). Peer-to-peer networks are typically designed in a way that independent remote entities mitigate the threat of hostile peers. In the Sybil attack, individuals present several identities simultaneously to gain unreasonably large influence over the system, and thus a hostile peer overcomes the power of friendly peers (Douceur, 2002). In other words, when one actor should present only node at a time, several nodes are controlled by a single person. In these attacks, the system cannot tell whether the tasks in the systems are distributed to different remote entities. As a result, attackers can block honest nodes from partaking in the system and can even control the majority of the voting power (51% attack) in a large-scale sybil attack. A typical solution to the problem is to rely on a trusted identification authority, but, as many cryptocurrencies are built on the idea of decentralization and trustlessness, these systems are typically designed to avoid the need to trust any identification authorities and are thus vulnerable to sybil attacks.

Proof of work and proof of stake are classic examples of how blockchains have designed avoiding sybil attacks. Here, it is considered that an independent remote entity needs to work or put something at stake to partake in the system. As a result, the friendliness to the system is proven. While this is not enough to avoid sybil attacks, these consensus mechanisms make the attacks impractical (difficult and expensive) (*Sybil Attacks Explained*, 2020).

Eclipse attacks

Eclipse attacks are attempts to isolate certain users from the network rather than attacking the whole system (as in sybil attacks). By isolating the user from the network, the victim cannot see the current picture of the real network and the ledger. This is possible as cryptocurrencies limit the number of outgoing connections. By default, bitcoin node randomly picks eight nodes to establish connections. By hijacking all these connections, an attacker can control the victim's connections and take advantage by, for instance, carrying out a 0 confirmation double-spend attack. In other words, they resend already spent coins to an isolated user. This is also possible as a so-called N-confirmation double-spending in which a merchant requires a certain amount of confirmations before accepting the transaction. If the attacker sends the transaction to eclipsed miners, it is possible to show their confirmations to the eclipsed merchant. The merchant sees the true ledger only after sending the goods.

In addition to $0/N$ confirmation double-spending, Heilman et al. (2015) discuss engineering block races and selfish mining that are possible through eclipse attacks. A block race happens, when a block is mined simultaneously by two miners. The other block will be followed, and the other will be "orphaned." Thus, an eclipse attack can be used for directing the eclipsed miners to waste effort on orphan blocks and thus engineer the block race. With selfish mining, by eclipsing other miners, the eclipse attacker changes the perception of the ratio of mining power controlled by the attacker to the honest mining power that will mine on the attacker's blocks during a block race. Thus, the attacker is able to win more than a fair share of the mining reward.

Eclipse attacks are relatively easy to conduct in structured networks when attackers can run several nodes from the same IP address. As a result, Marcus et al. (2018) argue that it is easier to conduct eclipse attack on the Ethereum network than it is on bitcoin. Therefore, it is possible to avoid eclipse attacks through random node selection, limiting the number of nodes from a single IP address, white labeling nodes and increasing the number of outgoing connections, which would make it more probable that a node is not eclipsed from the network. Recently, Xu et al. (2020) introduced a design for an eclipse attack detection model that identifies malicious actors in the network.

Spam attacks

A spam attack is the introduction of several simultaneous, small transactions that decelerate the network, delay the creation of new blocks in the blockchain and result loss of the computing power for maintaining the system for real transactions. Spam attacks diminish the number of connected peers in the system and may also result in network outage (Moubarak et al., 2018). While these attacks may be vulnerable to the system, it is not always easy to identify unnecessary transactions.

Over the years, there have been rumors on spam attacks on bitcoin (Suberg, 2019) and Ethereum (Memoria, 2018). While it is not always clear if there has been a real spam attack, it is clear that the average fees and block sizes have spiked from the introduction of small transactions in the network. This illuminates the potential vulnerability of cryptocurrencies to spam attacks.

Transaction fees are one way of avoiding spam attacks, as the fees make attacks expensive. For instance, bitcoin prioritizes high-fee transactions. However, many cryptocurrencies are designed to enable inexpensive transactions. In these systems, other methods are needed to prioritize legitimate transactions over spam. For instance, cryptocurrencies may introduce larger block sizes to decrease the burden of spam transactions. IOTA, on the other hand, requires that all transactions require PoW to secure two other transactions. As a result, spammers are incentivized to partake in the systems, as they increase the speed and security of the system (*IOTA Spam Fund*, 2020). However, this may increase the difficulty of mining and thus cause economic burden of keeping up the system. Some other cryptocurrencies have two mechanisms for different tiers, similar to nightclubs: no transaction fees for users with high reputations and transaction fees for nonpriority users.

GitHub attacks

GitHub attacks are probably the least known attacks presented in this chapter. They refer to the attacks made on GitHub, the software development platform used for many cryptocurrency projects in order to misuse the developers for personal intentions. In brevity, a charismatic person can take over a cryptocurrency and introduce several things that would benefit the individual but not necessarily improve the viability of the project.

There can be both technical and social solutions for preventing GitHub attacks. Nevertheless, operationalizing them in practice may be challenging. For instance, one could tie the suggestion power to the voting power, which would guarantee that the miners are taken into consideration in the development. This could result in large miners taking over the development work. As another example, there could be rules for limiting the new suggestions by a single individual. However, the real identities are not always known on GitHub. Moreover, these rules might slow down the development process, as the activities of the most active and sincere people ae hindered.

Conclusion

In this chapter, we have presented several sources of cybersecurity threats that are common in the field of cryptocurrency. We highlight that too many cryptocurrency projects still rely on trust and good faith in lead developers and pools. As a contribution, we bring together ideas from academic literature on the most common threats and introduce the discussion on GitHub attacks, which is a less known cybersecurity threat in cryptocurrency. Particularly, we hope that the chapter helps people in making their own research on whether it is safe to buy and use certain cryptocurrencies. While many of the threats can be solved by developers, it is important that cryptocurrency users are able to assess how well the system has been designed against the most common security threats.

In this chapter, we focused on 51% attacks, sybil attacks, eclipse attacks, spam attacks and GitHub attacks. While there is some academic literature on the first four attacks, it is important to have more studies that would describe how these attacks have been prevented and how they can be avoided in the future by designing more robust systems.

Moreover, we call for more research on cybersecurity threats in cryptocurrency. It is important to identify the threats and to develop solutions to these threats. Many of the threats in cryptocurrency, particularly in more centralized systems, are social by nature. Therefore, it would be important to develop technical solutions making cryptocurrencies less vulnerable to individual misbehavior.

References

Atzei, N., Bartoletti, M., and Cimoli, T. (2017). A survey of attacks on ethereum smart contracts (SoK). In M. Maffei and M. Ryan (eds.), *Principles of Security and Trust. POST 2017. Lecture Notes in Computer Science* (Vol. 10204). Berlin, Heidelberg: Springer.

Bastiaan, M. (2015). Preventing the 51%-attack: A stochastic analysis of two phase proof of work in Bitcoin, 10. Retrieved from http://referaat.cs.utwente.nl/conference/22/paper/7473/preventing-the-51-attack-a-stochastic-analysis-of-two-phase-proof-of-work-in-bitcoin.pdf.

Chen, H., Pendleton, M., Njilla, L., and Xu, S. (2019). A survey on ethereum systems security: Vulnerabilities, attacks and defenses. *ArXiv*, 1–29. Retrieved from http://arxiv.org/abs/1908.04507.

Cost of a 51% Attack. (2020). Retrieved January 13, 2020, from https://gobitcoin.io/.

Crypto 51. (2020). Retrieved January 13, 2020, from www.crypto51.app/.

Douceur, J. R. (2002). The Sybil attack. In *International Workshop on Peer-to-Peer Systems* (pp. 251–260). Berlin, Heidelberg: Springer. https://doi.org/10.1145/984622.984660.

Europol. (2019). Internet organised crime threat assessment (IOCTA). *IOCTA Report*, 1–63. Retrieved from www.europol.europa.eu/sites/default/files/documents/iocta2018.pdf.

Gervais, A., Karame, G. O., Wüst, K., Glykantzis, V., Ritzdorf, H., and Čapkun, S. (2016). On the security and performance of proof of work blockchains. In *Proceedings of Conference on Computer and Communications Security* (pp. 3–16). Retrieved from https://bitcoin.org/en/developer-reference#data-messages.

Heilman, E., Kendler, A., Zohar, A., and Goldberg, S. (2015). Eclipse attacks on Bitcoin's peer-to-peer network. *USENIX Security Symposium*, August, 129–144.

IOTA Spam Fund. (2020). Retrieved from https://ecosystem.iota.org/projects/iota-spam-fund.

Li, X., Jiang, P., Chen, T., Luo, X., and Wen, Q. (2017). A survey on the security of blockchain systems. *Future Generation Computer Systems*. https://doi.org/10.1016/j.future.2017.08.020.

Marcus, Y., Heilman, E., and Goldberg, S. (2018). Low-resource eclipse attacks on ethereum's peer-to-peer network. *IACR Cryptology EPrint Archive*, January, 236.

Memoria, F. (2018). *EOS Whales Behind Spam Attack on Ethereum Network, Claims DApp Developer*. Retrieved from www.cryptoglobe.com/latest/2018/07/os-whales-behind-spam-attack-on-ethereum-network-claims-dapp-developer/.

Moubarak, J., Filiol, E., and Chamoun, M. (2018). On blockchain security and relevant attacks. *2018 IEEE Middle East and North Africa Communications Conference, MENA-COMM 2018*, 1–6. https://doi.org/10.1109/MENACOMM.2018.8371010.

Otte, P., de Vos, M., and Pouwelse, J. (2017). TrustChain: A Sybil-resistant scalable blockchain. *Future Generation Computer Systems*. https://doi.org/10.1016/j.future.2017.08.048.

Saad, M., Spaulding, J., Njilla, L., Kamhoua, C., Shetty, S., Nyang, D., and Mohaisen, A. (2019). Exploring the attack surface of blockchain: A systematic overview, 1–30. Retrieved from http://arxiv.org/abs/1904.03487.

Suberg, W. (2019). Spam attack? Bitcoin average block size suddenly spikes to over 3MB. Retrieved January 13, 2020, from https://cointelegraph.com/news/spam-attack-bitcoin-average-block-size-suddenly-spikes-to-over-3mb.

Sybil Attacks Explained. (2020). Retrieved January 13, 2020, from www.binance.vision/security/sybil-attacks-explained.

Xu, G., Guo, B., Su, C., Zheng, X., Liang, K., Wong, D. S., and Wang, H. (2020). Am I eclipsed? A smart detector of eclipse attacks for Ethereum. *Computers and Security*, 88, 101604. https://doi.org/10.1016/j.cose.2019.101604.

Zhu, L., Zheng, B., Shen, M., Yu, S., Gao, F., Li, H., . . . Gai, K. (2018). *Research on the Security of Blockchain Data: A Survey*. Retrieved from http://arxiv.org/abs/1812.02009.

7 Cryptocurrencies and entrepreneurial finance

Pierluigi Martino, Cristiano Bellavitis and Carlos M. DaSilva

Introduction

Entrepreneurial firms, particularly young and innovative ones, need a large amount of capital to support their development, growth and ultimate success. These firms often require access to external sources of financing due to the lack of internal resources (Carpenter & Petersen, 2002). Nevertheless, new ventures may face difficulties in attracting external debt and traditional bank debt sources, owing to the capital market imperfections linked to the asymmetric information and the related adverse selection and moral hazard problems, which in turn limit their growth and jeopardize their survival (Berger & Udell, 1998; Cassar, 2004; Bruton et al., 2015).

Entrepreneurial finance literature has emphasized the importance of key mechanisms that provide the necessary financial resources for these companies (Bruton et al., 2015; Bellavitis et al., 2017; Block et al., 2018). Particularly the emergence of new innovation technologies is offering new financing alternatives for such ventures, thereby bringing potential opportunities as well as new risks. Within this context, a key innovation consists of cryptocurrencies and the underlying blockchain technology (Howell et al., 2018; Fisch, 2019). In particular, through the initial coin offerings (ICOs) mechanism, an innovative blockchain-based model, new ventures are raising money from the public in a peer-to-peer manner by selling their own cryptocurrency to a crowd of investors (Bellavitis et al., in press; Tapscott & Tapscott, 2017; Howell et al., 2018; Fisch, 2019).

Recent studies (Adhami et al., 2018; Block et al., 2018; Howell et al., 2018; Fisch, 2019; Martino et al., 2019) have acknowledged the potential of blockchain, cryptocurrencies and ICOs in the entrepreneurial finance context. These new innovations may offer entrepreneurs and investors interesting theoretical opportunities, including wider access to credit, availability of up-to-date information, reduced costs and information asymmetry in addition to posing strategic, regulatory and law enforcement challenges (EBA, 2017).

Nevertheless, to date, there is not a clear understanding of the potential of blockchain, cryptocurrencies and ICOs in the entrepreneurial finance context, since the literature is still in its infancy. The objective of this chapter is to explore how cryptocurrencies and the underlying blockchain technology affect entrepreneurship, by providing an overview on the ICO phenomenon and outlining its advantages and risks.

Initial coin offerings: a new fund-raising mechanism

ICOs are a new form of fund-raising from the public that leverages the power of cryptocurrencies and the underling blockchain technology (PwC, 2018; OECD, 2018). Specifically, ICOs work similarly to equity crowdfunding, however, its offering has a different nature – i.e., tokens – and uses blockchain technology for verification instead of crowdfunding platforms (Arnold et al., 2019). Thus, an ICO allocates tokens instead of shares to early investors in a business. They typically do not represent actual ownership in the company but often provide access to a venture's own ecosystem and can be traded on an aftermarket.

After the first ICO conducted in July 2013 by Mastercoin, a digital currency built on bitcoin's blockchain, thousands of ICOs have been successfully completed over the years, with the funding amounts in most ICOs exceeding most investment rounds by traditional funding vehicles (Schückes & Gutmann, 2020). For instance, in early 2018, EOS, a blockchain-based system that enables the development, hosting and execution of commercial-scale decentralized applications (dApps), raised USD 4.2 billion, exceeding the value of all but two IPOs sold worldwide in the same year (Howell et al., 2018). It represents one of the largest cryptocurrency fund-raisings to date, together with Telegram, a blockchain-based messaging service to enhance messenger ecosystem, which in March 2018 raised USD 1.7 billion in a presale. Another example of a successful ICO belongs to the Swiss project Tezos, which raised approximately USD 232 million in July 2017 for developing smart contracts and a decentralized governance platform.

The ICO market has seen a significant growth over the years, with more than USD 28.0 billion raised in 1,601 ICO campaigns in the period from 2013 to 2018 (Masiak et al., 2019). Also, as shown in the latest report (2019) by Strategy&, PwC's strategy consulting team, in the first ten months of 2019, more than 380 token offerings were successfully completed, managing to raise USD 4.1 billion. Thus, with a volume of USD 31 billion, ICO represents a key player in the entrepreneurial finance context as a new financing instrument for new start-ups.

ICOs: advantages and risks

It has largely been acknowledged that ICOs have a huge potential to shape the entrepreneurial finance landscape in the future (Block et al., 2018; Howell et al., 2018). Several scholars (Tapscott & Tapscott, 2017; Howell et al., 2018; Fisch, 2019) point out that ICOs may offer several advantages for both investors and new ventures by providing a new way to raise funds in a straightforward and fast way that is also cheaper than traditional funding mechanisms.

One of the key features of an ICO is that it works on a distributed ledger technology or blockchain. Above all, this enables new ventures to expand their funding opportunities compared to traditional crowdfunding. In particular, since a company has the possibility to issue securities directly on the ledger, they may have access to a broader pool of investors (ECB, 2016). Also, the cross-border nature of blockchain technology means that private investors around the world are able to participate in an ICO, thus increasing the number of potential investors in the company and consequently the potential amount of capital raised. Second, while traditional crowdfunding systems use central platforms hosted and managed by a third-party provider (i.e., crowdfunding platforms and banks) acting as trusted third parties responsible for collecting and redistributing the funds, the blockchain technology enables operations to be conducted in a decentralized peer-to-peer (P2P) network, where transactions are verified by a network-wide consensus mechanism, thus eliminating the need for the intermediary to verify transactions (Arnold et al., 2019). In particular, ICOs do not rely on a centralized organization to manage the network, but instead they are run in decentralized manner as so–called peer platforms (peer platform markets) by aggregating the contributions of a distributed network of peers, where coordination is provided by a set of rules encoded in the blockchain-based platform. Nevertheless, it is worth mentioning that a new variant of ICOs has recently emerged, namely initial exchange offerings (IEOs), which introduces a centralized authority. Specifically, IEOs rely on cryptocurrency exchanges to ensure the trustworthiness of potential projects and to connect high-quality projects to potential investors (Chen & Bellavitis, 2020).

Further, since ICOs do not have a specific regulatory framework with rules or platform policies to be considered when doing them, this lack of regulation gives companies great flexibility when raising funds and enables start-ups to raise large amounts of funding with minimal effort while avoiding the costs of compliance and intermediaries (Fisch, 2019). Thus, in addition to the possibility to collect capital from a large number of investors, the ICO may also enable cost reductions included in fund-raising, particularly due to the elimination of the middleman such as platforms or financial institutions. This means that ICOs may improve the efficiency of raising money, thus lowering the cost of capital for entrepreneurs and investors, since it offers a high-speed and low-cost way of collecting money – compared to other traditional mechanisms such as crowdfunding – for entrepreneurial activity.

Furthermore, according to Tapscott and Tapscott (2017), ICOs may democratize participation in global capital markets by allowing anyone to invest any amount in a company,[1] thus dramatically reducing entry barriers to participate financially in the successes of the start-up sector. Block et al. (2018, p. 246) concur, arguing that these innovations may "provide new ways to assess risk and treat financial information, allow for easier participation of non-professional investors in entrepreneurial financing, provide greater liquidity, and reduce monitoring costs of investors." This means that, through ICOs, small investors also may become involved and invest in projects they consider worthy.

Another advantage concerns the way in which the project is being funded, i.e., the medium sold, namely tokens. Depending on the type of token issued, in addition to the profit deriving from the company's success, investors may also speculate on the underlying cryptocurrency (Arnold et al., 2019). This means that investors may benefit from any additional revenue that might derive from the subsequent appreciation in value of their shares, namely cryptocurrencies.

Nevertheless, like any radically new innovation, ICOs have some shortcomings that may bring several risks linked particularly to the lack of regulation and the consequent lack of investor protection (Tapscott & Tapscott, 2017). The European Securities and Market Authority (ESMA) identified five potential risks deriving from investing in a ICO: (1) unregulated space, vulnerable to fraud or illicit activities, (2) high risk of losing all of the invested capital, (3) lack of exit options and extreme price volatility, (4) inadequate information and (5) flaws in the technology (ESMA, 2017).

First, the ESMA stresses the fact that ICOs are currently not regulated. As a result, investors cannot benefit from the protection that laws and regulations provide for them in the event that ICOs are used for fraudulent or illicit activities or for money laundering purposes. Indeed, the absence of regulation leads to an increased investment risk due to malignant behavior, since tokens often have no current counter-value and do not lead to any legal entitlement (Fisch, 2019). Moreover, since different countries have varying levels of regulatory strictness for ICOs, this may lead to vulnerabilities in the market (EY, 2017).

Second, since the majority of ICOs are launched by businesses that are at a very early stage of development, this implies an inherently high risk of failure, which in turn may lead investors to face a high risk of losing all of their invested capital. The ESMA also highlights the high volatility of the price of the coin or token, as well as the risk for investors to be exposed to the lack of exit options or to not being able to redeem their coin or token for a prolonged period, which may imply potential losses for investors.

Another risk concerns the lack of information made available to investors in the so-called white papers, which typically put the emphasis on the potential benefits but not on the risks of the projects, thus making investors not fully aware of the potential risks.

Finally, the ESMA points out the potential risks deriving from the flaws in the technology – i.e., blockchain – which may be subject to cyberattacks (i.e., cyber risks). Indeed, although it has largely been acknowledged that blockchain is secure, there have been several hacks and cyber-attacks over the years: as EY (2017) reported, more than 10 percent of ICO funds are lost or stolen in hacker attacks (almost USD 400 million).

Conclusion

The benefits of blockchain technology, cryptocurrencies and initial coin offerings (ICOs) are becoming increasingly apparent to entrepreneurial firms and investors, as well as to the public and major players in the international markets. Scholars and financial players have acknowledged the huge potential of these innovations in shaping the entrepreneurial finance landscape in the future (Block et al., 2018; Howell et al., 2018). By relying on blockchain technology, ICOs can reduce the friction in fund-raising, ease access to capital and thereby promote entrepreneurship and innovation (Chen & Bellavitis, 2020).

Recent studies have started to explore the ICO phenomenon by analyzing the geographic distribution of the ICOs (Huang et al., 2019) and investigating the determinants of an ICO success (e.g., Howell et al., 2018; Fisch, 2019). Nevertheless, literature is still fuzzy on the potential of ICOs for entrepreneurial finance (Block et al., 2018); thus more research is needed. For instance, future studies may investigate the effectiveness of ICOs in terms of their returns and successes after the offerings, as well as their consequent ability to foster entrepreneurship. The latter is critical since there is a lack information about whether the new players are reducing the early-stage funding gap in the financing of innovative ventures (Block et al., 2018). Research on the role played by the human and social capital of the founders is also needed in explaining ICOs outcomes (e.g., performance). Moreover, other studies could explore which business models (in addition to those based on blockchain and distributed ledger technology) are suitable to be funded by ICOs.

Note

1 Regarding this point, it is worth mentioning that some countries (e.g., China and South Korea) have banned token fund-raising.

References

Adhami, S., Giudici, G., and Martinazzi, S. (2018). Why do businesses go crypto? An empirical analysis of initial coin offerings. *Journal of Economics and Business*, 100, 64–75.

Arnold, L. et al. (2019). Blockchain and initial coin offerings: Blockchain's implications for crowdfunding. In H. Treiblmaier and R. Beck (eds.), *Business Transformation Through Blockchain*. Cham: Palgrave Macmillan.

Bellavitis, C., Cumming, D. J., and Vanacker, T. R. (in press). Ban, Boom, and Echo! Entrepreneurship and initial coin offerings. *Entrepreneurship Theory and Practice*.

Bellavitis, C., Filatotchev, I., Kamuriwo, D. S., and Vanacker, T. (2017). Entrepreneurial finance: New frontiers of research and practice: Editorial for the special issue Embracing entrepreneurial funding innovations. *Venture Capital*, 19 (1–2), 1–16.

Berger, A. N., and Udell, G. F. (1998). The economics of small business finance: The roles of private equity and debt markets in the financial growth cycle. *Journal of Banking & Finance*, 22 (6–8), 613–673.

Block, J. H., Colombo, M. G., Cumming, D. J., and Vismara, S. (2018). New players in entrepreneurial finance and why they are there. *Small Business Economics*, 50 (2), 239–250.

Bruton, G., Khavul, S., Siegel, D., and Wright, M. (2015). New financial alternatives in seeding entrepreneurship: Microfinance, crowdfunding, and peer-to-peer innovations. *Entrepreneurship Theory and Practice*, 39 (1), 9–26.

Carpenter, R. E., and Petersen, B. C. (2002). Is the growth of small firms constrained by internal finance? *Review of Economics and Statistics*, 84 (2), 298–309.

Cassar, G. (2004). The financing of business start-ups. *Journal of Business Venturing*, 19 (2), 261–283.

Chen, Y., and Bellavitis, C. (2020). Blockchain disruption and decentralized finance: The rise of decentralized business models. *Journal of Business Venturing Insights*, 13, e00151.

EBA (European Banking Authority). (2017). *Discussion Paper on the EBA's Approach to Financial Technology (FinTech)*. Retrieved from https://eba.europa.eu/eba-publishes-a-discussion-paper-on-its-approach-to-fintech.

ECB (European Central Bank). (2016). Distributed ledger technology. *Financial Technology & Automated Investing* (1).

ESMA. (2017). ESMA highlights ICO risks for investors and firms. Retrieved from www.esma.europa.eu/press-news/esma-news/esma-highlights-ico-risks-investors-and-firms.

EY. (2017). EY research: Initial coin offerings (ICOs). December. Retrieved from www.ey.com/Publication/vwLUAssets/ey-research-initial-coin-offerings-icos/$File/ey-research-initial-coin-offerings-icos.pdf.

Fisch, C. (2019). Initial coin offerings (ICOs) to finance new ventures. *Journal of Business Venturing*, 34 (1), 1–22.

Howell, S. T., Niessner, M., and Yermack, D. (2018). *Initial Coin Offerings: Financing Growth with Cryptocurrency Token Sales* (No. w24774). NBER Working Papers 24774, National Bureau of Economic Research.

Huang, W., Meoli, M., and Vismara, S. (2019). The geography of initial coin offerings. *Small Business Economics*, 1–26.

Martino, P., Wang, K. J., Bellavitis, C., and DaSilva, C. (2019). An introduction to blockchain, cryptocurrency and initial coin offerings. In A Quas. et al. (eds.), *New Frontiers of Entrepreneurial Finance*. Singapore: World Scientific.

Masiak, C., Block, J. H., Masiak, T., Neuenkirch, M., and Pielen, K. N. (2019). Initial coin offerings (ICOs): Market cycles and relationship with Bitcoin and ether. *Small Business Economics*, 1–18.

OECD. (2018). *Blockchain Technology and Corporate Governance*. Retrieved from www.oecd.org/officialdocuments/publicdisplaydocumentpdf/?cote=DAF/CA/CG/RD(2018)1/REV1&docLanguage=En.

PwC. (2018). *Understanding the ICO*. Retrieved from http://usblogs.pwc.com/emerging-technology/understanding-the-ico-infographic/.

PwC. (2019). *6th ICO/STO Report. A Strategic Perspective*. Retrieved from www.pwc.ch/en/publications/2020/Strategy&_ICO_STO_Study_Version_Spring_2020.pdf.

Schückes, M., and Gutmann, T. (2020). Why do startups pursue initial coin offerings (ICOs)? The role of economic drivers and social identity on funding choice. *Small Business Economics*, 1–26.

Tapscott, A., and Tapscott, D. (2017). How blockchain is changing finance. *Harvard Business Review*, 1.

8 Crowdfunding and initial coin offerings

Jean-Marie Ayer and Bruno Pasquier

Introduction

The combination of crowdfunding, a financing method exponentially growing in recent years, and emerging blockchain-based technologies opens up revolutionary financing opportunities for start-ups and small and medium-sized companies (SMEs). Beginning with the history of crowdfunding, this chapter argues that blockchain technology enables start-ups and SMEs to raise funds from a multitude of investors on a peer-to-peer basis without the involvement of an intermediary. Next, the phenomenon of initial coin offerings (ICOs) is discussed and illustrated with concrete examples. Finally, the current legal framework governing ICOs is reviewed.

ICOs as a new type of crowdfunding

Crowdfunding – definition and applications

Crowdfunding is by definition "a collective effort by people who network and pool their money together, usually via the Internet, in order to invest in and support efforts initiated by other people or organizations" (Ordanini et al., 2011, p. 443). While the concept of crowdfunding has arguably been around for centuries,[1] it acquires a new meaning in the current economic, social and technological contexts. The combination of new technologies, e-commerce and online peer communities creates an entirely new decentralized space where individuals play an increasingly influential role.

The term "crowdfunding" is related to the broader trends of "crowdsourcing," "co-production" and "sharing economy," wherein assets and knowledge are made available and accessed by online communities. First coined by Jeff Howe (2006), the term was then quickly adopted. From 2008 onwards, the academic research that followed has given rise to many studies resulting in numerous and sometimes contradictory interpretations and definitions of the term, as explained by Estellés-Arolas and Guevara (2012). The two authors proposed a comprehensive definition of crowdsourcing, including the following main components: a task proposed by an organization; a community willing to undertake the task voluntarily; an online environment to mediate the engagement of the community; and mutual benefits for both the organization proposing a task and for the community contributing to the solution.

Along with the growth of crowdsourcing, the sharing economy represents another fast-developing, IT-mediated form of economic functioning. Referring to a process providing users with temporary access to tangible and intangible resources that may be crowdsourced (Eckhardt et al., 2019), this emerging paradigm has been growing continuously in the last decade, supported by the proliferation of Internet-based, peer-to-peer services in a wide range of economic sectors, such as accommodation sharing (e.g., Airbnb), car sharing (e.g., Sharoo), ride sharing (e.g., BlaBlaCar), performing everyday tasks (e.g., Task-Rabbit) and crowdfunding (e.g., Kickstarter).

Sharing economy scholars conceptualize the sharing economy as a "system" in which customers take on enhanced roles as both providers and users of resources. This two-sided role, instead of a one-sided consumer role, also gives rise to new theoretical frameworks on collaborative consumption (e.g., Ertz et al., 2019; Hamari et al., 2016).

The new ecosystem created by the sharing economy and the dual role of the consumer have also seen the growth of projects funded by crowds. The consumer's role expands to "the investment support and the study of the reasons to pay for producing and promoting a product instead of buying it, and bear the risk associated with that decision" (Ordanini et al., 2011, p. 443). In the beginning, crowdfunding was mainly used to finance artists from different sectors (e.g., Brabham, 2008; Agrawal et al., 2013). Using crowdfunding Internet platforms (e.g., ArtistShare, SellaBand), musicians could seek donations from their fans to produce digital recordings and make their creative work available to the public by their own means through the Internet network. This form of financing and distribution has been attractive for musicians seeking to become less dependent on record companies and had a disruptive effect on those traditional intermediaries, like Universal Music Group and Sony BMG (Manovich, 2009).

Subsequently, more rewards-based crowdfunding platforms were launched, such as Indiegogo in 2008 and Kickstarter in 2009, hosting campaigns for other artistic and creative areas (e.g., fine art, photography) and social causes (e.g., animals, health). Those who financially contribute to a project are generally rewarded with a perk whose value depends on their contribution.

Funding companies through the crowd has been discussed intensively since 2010 and explored in practice and theory. In the early phases of a company's life cycle (pre-seed/seed stage), the founders provide funding themselves or get it from friends and family, and if possible, from business angels. Funding from venture capitalists and banks is usually available only in the later development phases of start-ups (Robb & Robinson, 2014). Crowdfunding is seen as a way to reduce the funding gap in the early stages of new ventures (Hemer et al., 2011; Meinshausen et al., 2012; Agrawal et al., 2013).

ICOs – the rise of a new type of crowdfunding

The advent of blockchain technology with the launch of bitcoin in 2009 brought a new wave of decentralization. As a distributed public ledger managed by a peer-to-peer network, blockchain can be used to record transactions between two parties without relying on any centralized server or intermediary, but instead on the agreement of every peer in the network collectively maintaining a list of records called blocks (Swan, 2015). The system allows the exchange of value without the need for a trusted central authority or intermediary (e.g., government, bank). Most recent developments in blockchain technologies also implement additional features allowing for the execution of computer programs on top of a distributed ledger (smart contracts), thereby extending the system for the deployment of contractual transactions without third parties (Swan, 2015).

Using the potential of distributed ledger technologies (DLTs), ICOs (also called "token launches" or "generations") have recently emerged as a novel mechanism for financing entrepreneurial ventures. The term describes the creation and distribution of digital tokens by companies to investors, in exchange for fiat currency or first-generation cryptocurrencies, such as bitcoin or Ether (Naskar & Pasquier, 2018). The sale of tokens by the issuer provides capital to fund the initial development of the venture. The raising of 5,000 bitcoins in 2013 (worth USD 500,000 in 2013) in the Mastercoin project is considered to be the first ICO (Abraham, 2018). Between January 2014 and June 2018, ICOs raised over USD 18 billion (Howell et al., 2018). Often, ICOs take place in countries with advantageous taxation and nonrigid FinTech regulations.[2]

Despite their initial success, ICOs were rapidly perceived as lacking investor protection, such as granting security to token holders, rights to dividends or other predefined revenue streams. Two new types of token offerings emerged in 2019 to supplement the ICO and provide additional investor protection.

The first type is a security token offering (STO), which is a sale of tokens with features comparable to standard regular securities fully regulated and approved within at least one jurisdiction. STOs are an alternative to regular token sales (ICOs). Under an STO, the tokens are fully backed by securities and other stakeholder obligations regarding token distribution, issuance procedure and secondary trades.

The second type is an initial exchange offering (IEO), which is an ICO (or STO) exclusively operated on the platform of a cryptocurrency exchange. The crypto exchange administers the IEO on behalf of the company that raises funds using newly issued tokens. This option essentially provides an advantage to the investors who can process know-your-customer and anti–money laundering (KYC/AML) only once on their preferred exchange instead of multiple KYC processes for each ICO/STO.

ICOs, STOs and IEOs are alternatives to classic debt- or capital-funding as performed today by venture capital or private equity firms and banks. As such, we can view them as a new value transfer mechanism, promoting financing of economic activities through disintermediation.

Evolution and examples of ICOs

In general, crowdfunding campaigns involve a limited degree of disintermediation, given the participation of a professional intermediary for marketing and fund-raising. The DLT could help fund-raisers go one step further. Going back to the previous example, artists using blockchain-based crowdfunding can enter transactions with the audience on a peer-to-peer basis without the involvement of intermediary operators collecting and distributing funds (De Filippi, 2016). Relevant in this case is not only the decentralized nature of DLT but also the way rewards for backers are potentially generated through tokens. Backers can be rewarded with a share or vested interest in the project they are supporting. It creates a more balanced relationship between those who are promoting the project and those who are contributing financial resources to it. The implications of the use of cryptoasset-based crowdfunding for artistic creation could mean that the public is no more a passive consumer but instead an active stakeholder in cultural creation.

The relevance of vested interest from backers in crowdfunding processes can be further illustrated with the example of Ambrosus, which conducted one of the major Swiss ICOs in 2017. The objective of the project was to build a blockchain-based ecosystem targeting the supply chain industry with an emphasis on "life-essential products," in particular food and pharmaceuticals (Ambrosus, n.d.). The token, Amber, which was issued to the participants in this ICO, is used for all transactions within the Ambrosus network. The token pursues a dual purpose: (1) binding data that are generated or collected through the network and (2) transferring units of value within the ecosystem (Ambrosus, n.d.).

As items move through the supply chain, the Amber balance assigned to a particular tracked-batch splits into multiple smart contracts. All transactions together constitute the history graph of a given item. The Amber tokens remain bonded to a tracked item until a defined expiration date or the occurrence of a "termination event," like a purchase or delivery. At the end of the cycle, end consumers can claim the remaining balance of tokens bound to the final delivery of the product and use them again. This option incentivizes consumers to purchase Ambrosus-tracked products. In the example of Ambrosus, the token has a technical utility and derives its value from users of the network willing to use and operate the provided service.

Ambrosus was typical for early-stage ICOs that took place between 2014 and 2017. In early ICO projects, tokens often had an intrinsic value linked to the success of ambitious technological development associated to blockchain technologies and their applications. In all these projects, the tokens issued under the ICO are inseparable from the solution and the value promised to purchasers.

Third parties acquiring the cryptoassets are involved in the development and use of the solution.

More recently, another type of ICOs has come to the forefront. In this new type of ICO, the blockchain is nothing more than the technological backbone of a crowdfunding campaign, in which the issuing company promises a counterpart, which could also be delivered without using this technology. The blockchain serves only to facilitate the transfer of the counterpart and monitor the relationship between issuers and backers. The blockchain-based issuance of equity is the archetype of this new type of ICOs (in this case, the ICO is also called "STO"). The exchange on a distributed ledger is fast and secure and does not involve intermediation by banks (Pasquier & Ayer, 2019).

Regulation of ICOs

This new crowdfunding method also needs to comply with the regulatory framework in which it operates. Due to their rapid and important growth, ICOs have been a major focus for regulators over recent years. The most effective way for governments to regulate blockchain is to impose laws on end users – i.e., to issuers and purchasers of tokens, not to developers of blockchains (De Filippi & Wright, 2018).

One of the main challenges related to the legal regulation of ICOs is the functional diversity of the tokens issued in crowdfunding campaigns. Tokens can be linked to different types of rights, such as membership rights (shares or similar) or property rights. Accordingly, different legal rules apply to ICOs, depending on the tokens issued. Several classifications describe the possible functions of tokens, relevant for the regulation of the ICO. One common classification, used by the Swiss Financial Market Supervisory Authority (FINMA), distinguishes between payment tokens, utility tokens and asset tokens (FINMA, 2018). Payment tokens, commonly referred to as cryptocurrencies, have exclusively a payment function. Utility tokens provide access to a service or a product. Asset tokens are linked to underlying assets. Tokens can also combine different functions (hybrid tokens).

A key aspect regarding the financial market regulations of ICOs is whether the tokens qualify as securities (in this case, the ICO is also called "STO"). A fundamental problem for the said qualification lies in the different definitions, depending on the applicable jurisdictions. Pursuant to Article 4 of Directive 2014/65 of the European Union, securities mean "those classes of securities which are negotiable on the capital market, with the exception of instruments of payment." Pursuant to Article 3 lit. b) of the Swiss Financial Services Act, securities are standardized certificated and uncertificated securities, derivatives and intermediated securities, which are suitable for mass trading. In the United States, the definition of securities is broad and includes, for example, investment contracts (Rosenblum, 2003). To determine whether a token qualifies as a security, the U.S. Securities and Exchange Commission (SEC) applies the Howey test (SEC, 2017). According to the Howey test, "an investment contract is an investment of money in a common enterprise with a reasonable expectation of profits to be derived from the entrepreneurial or managerial efforts of others" (SEC, 2017, p. 11).

Because of the differences in the laws applicable to ICO crowdfunding campaigns previously mentioned, it is crucial to determine the applicable national law. However, due to the newness of blockchain, specific regulations in private international law codifications are missing (Guillaume, 2018). Therefore, the applicable law will depend on the law governing the contract or the issuance of a security. Under some jurisdictions, securities issued as tokens on the blockchain must be registered. In general, all securities offered in the United States must be registered with the SEC (SEC, 2011). In other jurisdictions, as in Switzerland, securities offered to the public do not need to be registered with a central entity. Furthermore, relevant jurisdictions will, in general, impose the release of a prospectus providing relevant information to the investors. Recently, the European Union Commission Delegated Regulation 2019/33 simplified the prospectus requirement in EU member states.

In a similar context, the issuance of tokens on the blockchain might be incompatible with further requirements imposed by the applicable law. For example, the definition of the term "stock ledger" in section 219 of the General Corporation Law of Delaware, U.S., was amended in 2017 to permit a record-keeping system utilizing blockchain databases. In Switzerland, the transfer of securities on a blockchain is not permitted under applicable law due to the requirement of a written and signed assignment (Pasquier & Ayer, 2019). If the tokens are, in addition, used as a means of payment, anti–money laundering regulations might apply (FINMA, 2018). If the tokens are used as financing instruments (e.g., with reimbursement or payment of dividends), the issuer might have to apply for a banking or similar license (FINMA, 2018).

Conclusion

This chapter shows that crowdfunding is not a recent phenomenon but has been around for centuries. In the early 2000s, this concept was discussed mainly in connection with the funding of artistic projects. However, digital technology and blockchain, in particular, are taking crowdfunding to a new level. Blockchain helps transactions on a peer-to-peer basis without the involvement of intermediary operators collecting funds. This contribution describes the evolution of ICOs, using concrete examples from essentially digital projects to projects in which blockchain simply facilitates, for example, the transfer of shares. Finally, the legal ICO framework is explored. Several regulations may apply to ICOs, especially if the tokens are considered to be securities. The legal difficulties are twofold: (1) depending on the applicable laws, the rules are different, and (2) so far, most national jurisdictions include only a few rules specific to blockchain technologies.

Notes

1 The *New York World* collected over USD 100,000 in donations – most donations being about USD 1 or less – to ensure the completion of the pedestal of the Statue of Liberty. Another case of crowdfunding was the issuance of notes by Auguste Comte in 1798 for the public support of his future work as a philosopher (Simons, 2016).
2 See the example of Swiss ICO Foundations discussed by Naskar and Pasquier (2018).

References

Abraham, S. (2018). *The Origin Story of the Initial Coin Offering (ICO) Token Sale History*. Retrieved from https://newconomy.media/news/the-origin-story-of-the-initial-coin-offering-ico-token-sale-history.

Agrawal Ajay, K., Catalini, C., and Goldfarb, A. (2013). *Some Simple Economics of Crowdfunding*. Nber Working Paper Series, Working Paper 19133.

Ambrosus. (n.d.). *Whitepaper*. Retrieved from https://ambrosus.com/assets/en/-White-Paper-V8-1.pdf.

Brabham, D. C. (2008). Crowdsourcing as a model for problem solving, an introduction and cases. *Convergence*, 14 (1), 75–90.

De Filippi, P. (2016). Blockchain-based Crowdfunding: what impact on artistic production and art consumption? Archive ouverte HAL. Retrieved from https://hal.archives-ouvertes.fr/hal-01265211/document.

De Filippi, P., and Wright, A. (2018). *Blockchain and the Law*. Cambridge, MA and London: Harvard University Press.

Eckhardt, G. M., Houston, M., Jiang, B., Lamberton, C., Rindfleisch, A., and Zervas, G. (2019). Marketing in the sharing economy. *Journal of Marketing*, 83 (5), 5–27.

Ertz, M., Durif, F., and Arcand, M. (2019). A conceptual perspective on collaborative consumption. *AMS Review*, 9, 27–41.

Estellés-Arolas, E., González, L., and Guevara, F. (2012). Towards an integrated crowdsourcing definition. *Journal of Information Science*, 38 (2), 189–200.

FINMA. (2018). Guidelines for enquiries regarding the regulatory framework for initial coin offerings (ICOs). February 1. Retrieved from www.finma.ch/en/news/2018/02/20180216-mm-ico-wegleitung/.

Guillaume, F. (2018). Blockchain: le pont du droit international privé entre l'espace numérique et l'espace physique. In Ilaria Pretelli (ed.), *Le droit international privé dans le labyrinthe des plateformes digitales* (pp. 163–189). Geneva, Basel and Zurich: Schulthess.

Hamari, J., Sjöklint, M., and Ukkonen, A. (2016). The sharing economy: Why people participate in collaborative consumption. *Journal of the Association for Information Science and Technology*, 67 (9), 2047–2059.

Hemer, J., Schneider, U., Dornbusch, F., and Frey, S. (2011). *Crowdfunding und andere Formen informeller Mikrofinanzierung in der Projekt- und Innovationsfinanzierung*. Stuttgart: Fraunhofer Verlag.

Howe, J. (2006). *Crowdsourcing: A Definition*. Retrieved from crowdsourcing.com.

Howell, S. T., Niessner, M., and Yermack, D. (2018). *Initial Coin Offerings: Financing Growth with Cryptocurrency Token Sales*. Working Paper Series, 24774, June, National Bureau of Economic Research.

Manovich, L. (2009). The practice of everyday (media) life: From mass consumption to mass cultural production? *Critical Inquiry*, 35 (2), 319–331.

Meinshausen, S., Schiereck, D., and Stimeier, S. (2012). Crowdfunding als Finanzierungs-alternative-Innovative Ansätze in der Unternehmensfinanzierung. *WiSt*, 11, November, 583–588.

Naskar, A., and Pasquier, B. (2018). The tale of Swiss ICO foundations advantages and limitation in the choice of the adequate legal form. *Aktuelle Juristische Praxis*, 1, 89-94.

Ordanini, A., Miceli, L., Pizzetti, M., and Parasuraman, A. (2011). Crowd-funding: Trans-forming customers into investors through innovative service platforms. *Journal of Service Management*, 22 (4), 443–470.

Pasquier, B., and Ayer, A. (2019). Formungültige Aktienübertragungen auf der Blockchain. *Anwaltsrevue*, 5, 196-202.

Robb, A., and Robinson, D. (2014). The capital structure decisions of new firms. *The Review of Financial Studies*, 27 (1), 153–179.

Rosenblum, R. H. (2003). *Investment Company Determination under the 1940 Act: Exemptions and Exceptions*. 2nd Edition. Chicago: Section of Business Law, American Bar Association.

SEC. (2011). Registration under the securities act of 1933. September 2. Retrieved from www.sec.gov/fast-answers/answersregis33htm.html.

SEC. (2017). Release No. 81207/July 25. Retrieved from www.sec.gov/litigation/investreport/34-81207.pdf.

Simons, O. (2016). *Crowdfunding Comte*. Retrieved from http://positivists.org/blog/archives/5959.

Swan, M. (2015). *Blockchain, Blueprint for a New Economy*. Beijing: O Reilly.

9 Cryptocurrencies and trade

Allison Derrick[1]

Cryptocurrencies have the potential to remove or reduce barriers to international trade by offering transactions with low or no processing fees, faster processing times and trust without an intermediary. Yet the potential of cryptocurrencies to replace traditional fiat currency is limited by their ability to act as a medium of exchange and store of value and their association with illegal activity. As economic activity facilitated by cryptocurrency grows, measuring its contribution to economic output and international trade becomes an important consideration to policy makers who must regulate and understand the economic impacts of this new financial instrument.

The thousands of cryptocurrencies that currently exist are best classified for economic accounting by whether they are mineable or nonmineable cryptocurrencies. If they are nonmineable, whether their value is tied to another underlying claim or asset is also important. These characteristics determine how the cryptocurrency derives value and how new coins are introduced into circulation. The resulting classes of cryptocurrency are summarized in Figure 9.1. For economic accounting purposes, these characteristics influence whether trade in cryptocurrencies is considered services in the current account, rent in the capital account or investment income in the financial account, which in turn determine cryptocurrencies' effect on GDP.

Mineable cryptocurrencies are the largest class of cryptocurrencies, as measured by market capitalization. In 2018, the total market capitalization of all cryptocurrencies was about USD 129 billion, of which 53 percent was claimed by bitcoin and 11 percent by Ether, both of which are mineable cryptocurrencies. Ripple, a leading nonmineable cryptocurrency, claimed 9 percent of total market capitalization (CoinMarketCap, n.d.). Transactions for mineable cryptocurrencies are cleared by miners who earn a new unit of currency and associated transaction fees. Currently, the value of all mineable cryptocurrencies, including bitcoin and Ether, reflects market supply and demand. Unlike fiat currencies, they do not represent a claim on their issuer or other underlying asset.

The next largest class of cryptocurrencies is nonmineable cryptocurrencies that are not backed by another underlying asset. This category includes coins like Ripple and EOS. Transactions are verified by a trusted network of

	Mineable	Non-mineable
Claim (backed by underlying asset)	None known	Non-mineable cryptocurrencies with a claim (NC) • Central bank digital currency: issued by a central bank or government • Fiat token: Backed by a reserve of fiat currency, e.g. Gemini, Tether USD • Investment coin: value is backed by non-fiat asset, e.g. Petro and Digital Swiss Gold
No claim (not backed by underlying asset)	Mineable cryptocurrencies without a claim (M) • Price determined by market and may be mined, e.g. Bitcoin and Ether	Non-mineable cryptocurrencies with no claim (NN) • Price determined by market but not mineable, e.g. Ripple

Figure 9.1 Types of cryptocurrencies

validators, who collect associated transaction fees. New coins for these types of cryptocurrencies are introduced into circulation by the issuer, and users must obtain new coins through a trade or purchase. In general, cryptocurrencies that are not backed by another underlying asset tend to be less stable in value than fiat currency.

The remaining nonmineable cryptocurrencies are backed by another underlying asset or claim on the issuer. When these cryptocurrencies are issued by a central bank or government, they are called central bank digital currencies (CBDCs) and are comparable to fiat currency. Currently, few CBDCs exist, so their potential benefits or drawbacks are mostly theoretical. When not issued by a central bank, asset-backed cryptocurrencies are called "stablecoins." The asset may be fiat currency, like the U.S. dollar or Japanese yen, or a noncurrency asset, like commodities or securities. Those backed by fiat currency are called "fiat tokens" and are intended to be a pure medium of exchange, like Tether USD and Gemini. Those backed by noncurrency assets are sometimes called investment coins, or "i-money" (Adrian & Mancini-Griffoli, 2019). Examples include Digital Swiss Gold and Novem, which are backed by gold.

To help policy makers gauge the usage of this new technology, international statistical agencies are studying the feasibility of accounting for cryptocurrency in their official economic statistics. This chapter examines the advantages and disadvantages of cryptocurrencies relative to fiat currencies in international transactions in order to provide context for my discussion of these accounting efforts. It then describes ongoing work to measure cryptocurrency transactions and discusses the source data necessary and available for this task.

Advantages of cryptocurrencies over fiat currencies in international transactions

The faster transactions, lower fees and higher transparency offered by cryptocurrencies can facilitate additional international transactions, such as some foreign worker remittances and cross-border payment settlements, that are currently too expensive or impossible using traditional fiat currency.

In the traditional banking system, cross-border payments clear in about three to seven days, while the same transaction using cryptocurrency can clear in as little as a few seconds. Figure 9.2 shows the current average transactions speed of common cryptocurrencies. Transactions using Ripple or Stellar Lumens are nearly instantaneous. In contrast, transactions using bitcoin Cash are the slowest, taking about 150 minutes to clear, and transactions in bitcoin and Zcash are also relatively slow at about 60 minutes.

Another benefit to users is that the fees associated with these transactions are usually lower than those of existing systems of clearing transactions. Customers using existing systems, such as the Society for Worldwide Interbank Financial Telecommunication (SWIFT), founded in 1973, accumulate relatively larger fees as transactions pass through intermediary banks. Senders in cryptocurrency

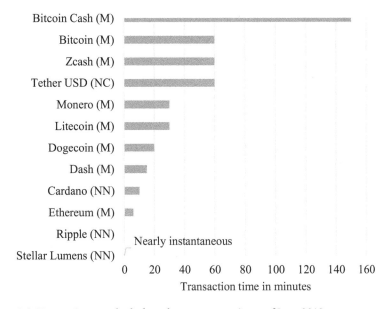

Figure 9.2 Transaction speed of selected cryptocurrencies as of June 2019

Source: Kraken.com

transactions typically pay a much smaller fee, which is collected by the miner or validator (for nonminable cryptocurrencies) of the transaction. For a sense of growth and scale, estimated revenues from bitcoin mining grew from USD 0.2 million in 2010 to more than USD 2 billion in 2016 (Hileman & Rauchs, 2017). Figure 9.3 shows the median transaction fee charged to senders in a selected group of currencies. Senders paid about USD 1.70 when using bitcoin, while those using bitcoin Cash, Ripple and Stellar Lumens paid a fee that is close to zero.

In economies with high inflation, frequent financial crises and capital or currency controls, cryptocurrencies may be more stable and liquid than domestic fiat currencies (Hileman, 2015). To illustrate this point, on the exchange Local-Bitcoins, which facilitates direct person-to-person exchange of fiat currency for cryptocurrency, usage was highest in Russia and Venezuela (Blandin et al., 2018). In these contexts, using cryptocurrency can improve a user's purchasing power over some fiat currencies.

Cryptocurrency can also facilitate smaller international transactions that would otherwise be too expensive. An application with a potentially large impact is worker remittances, which are often expensive to send through traditional money service providers (Hileman, 2015). Another application is paying for small freelance tasks in cryptocurrency through online peer-to-peer freelance markets like Fiverr and Upwork. In 2018, 46 percent of about 180 surveyed cryptocurrency payment services providers facilitated international remittances, and 33 percent facilitated micropayments (Blandin et al., 2018).

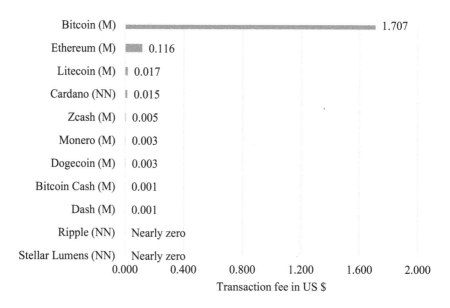

Figure 9.3 Median transaction fees for selected cryptocurrencies as of June 2019

Source: Coinmetrics.io

Some firms specialize in the settlement of legitimate cross-border payments by offering a cryptocurrency-based system to replace SWIFT. An early competitor in this area is Ripple, which hosts a cryptocurrency platform for its own coin, XPR, and which supports cryptocurrency or digital token systems built by others. Other options may soon be available. In 2019, Facebook announced plans for Libra, a cryptocurrency designed for peer-to-peer and customer-to-business transactions. Established banks are also testing proprietary cryptocurrency solutions, for example, JPM Coin for J.P. Morgan's institutional clients.

Disadvantages of cryptocurrencies over fiat currencies in international transactions

Despite the advantages it offers over fiat currencies, cryptocurrency is still limited in its ability to function as a currency and by its association with illegal activity.

Most cryptocurrencies fulfill only one of three key roles of currency (IMF, 2018; OECD, 2018). First, most business and individuals do not accept cryptocurrency as a medium of exchange for goods and services. Currently, its use is limited to a handful of Internet-based companies. The costs associated with accommodating a new payment method are likely high, especially when the infrastructure for credit and debit card payments is already in place. Second, the prices of most cryptocurrencies are volatile, and it is unclear whether they will stabilize in the future (Corbet et al., 2019), which undermines their use as a store of value. Moreover, users are exposed to significant price exchange risk relative to stable fiat currencies. Asset-backed cryptocurrencies may help to overcome this obstacle when their value is tied to another more stable asset but may be vulnerable to a loss of confidence in the currency. A third role of currency is to act as a unit of account, which means it must be fungible, divisible and countable. This is true of cryptocurrencies, but they are neither as liquid as fiat currency nor as stable in value, which reduces their usefulness as a unit of account.

Businesses creating or transacting in cryptocurrencies also face regulatory hurdles on issues such as the potential creation of new monopolies, risks to consumer protection and privacy, and monitoring systems for illegal activity. The remainder of this section focuses on the last hurdle – the relationship between cryptocurrency and illegal activity.

The relative anonymity of cryptocurrency may attract illegal activity. Cryptocurrency transactions are often less transparent than those in fiat currencies because the digital address used to make and receive payments is not directly linked to a personal identity or physical location. This anonymity makes verifying the identity of the other party in a transaction difficult for users and law enforcement. However, when the owner of a digital address is identified, this user's complete history of transactions is traceable on the public blockchain. Estimates of exactly how much illegal activity is facilitated through cryptocurrency are highly speculative. In some cases, they may also help circumvent economic sanctions by offering an alternative to bank financing. For example, in 2018, the Venezuelan government launched the largely unsuccessful oil-backed Petro cryptocurrency to help overcome sanctions imposed by the United States and the European Union. These associations with illegality may reduce the appeal of cryptocurrency for many users.

Traditional banks and payment systems discourage criminal activity by tying transactions to the sender's and recipient's identities. Under U.S. law, banks must monitor transactions to detect financial activity that appears illicit, like money laundering and tax evasion. Cryptocurrency exchanges, which are online platforms for buying and selling cryptocurrencies, are increasingly subject to similar laws like know-your-customer regulations (Blandin et al., 2018). As exchanges enforce these regulations, concerns about the use of cryptocurrencies in illegal activity may decline.

Cryptocurrencies in trade (balance of payments) accounting: concepts

Deciding how cryptocurrencies and their associated transactions should be classified in balance of payments accounting is key to measuring their contribution to international economic activity.

Cryptocurrencies' implications for economic accounting are currently being explored by international statistical agencies. Most of the discussion has focused on mineable currencies. The Organization for Economic Co-operation and Development (OECD) and the International Monetary Fund Statistics Department (IMFSD) produced papers discussing the economic accounting treatment options for mineable cryptocurrencies. Both papers support classifying cryptocurrencies as an asset because the currencies have clear ownership and owners can derive economic benefits by holding them over time (IMFSD, 2018; OECD, 2018). The rest of this section discusses whether cryptocurrencies should be considered (1) financial or nonfinancial assets and (2) produced or nonproduced assets.

Both papers argue that any cryptocurrency with a counterpart liability should be treated as a financial asset (IMFSD, 2018; OECD, 2018). This interpretation suggests that CBDCs, fiat tokens and investment coins are financial assets. Based on this argument, any unbacked cryptocurrencies should be classified as nonfinancial because they do not represent a claim on the issuer (IMFSD, 2018) and do not entitle the holder to receive an agreed sum at an agreed date (OECD, 2018).

However, fiat currencies are not clearly backed by a corresponding liability. Because gold and silver standards have largely been abandoned, fiat currency derives value from its holders' confidence in the currency and by virtue of being established by a central bank or government. Similarly, monetary gold does not come with a corresponding liability by the issuer but is classified as a financial asset due to trust and confidence in gold's value. Futures markets for fiat currency and gold manifest holders' belief in their value; some cryptocurrencies are also traded in futures markets. Unbacked cryptocurrencies may then derive their value similarly to fiat currency and monetary gold (OECD, 2018), which could justify their classification as financial assets.

Mineable cryptocurrencies are arguably produced assets because new coins are generated by mining, a production process requiring inputs of capital and labor (IMFSD, 2018; OECD, 2018). There are two potential ways to measure the output of mining activities. First, one could treat the mining of cryptocurrency like the mining of precious metals in the national accounts (IMFSD, 2018; OECD, 2018). Output is then recorded as the sum of the fee and the market value of the new coin in either the capital account as gross fixed capital formation or the financial account as a financial asset (OECD, 2018). Second, one could treat cryptocurrencies like fiat currency since they are intended to be used in the same way. Then the output of cryptocurrency mining should be treated like the production of fiat currency and recorded in the production account as the sum of production costs (OECD, 2018). The first option is likely more practical to implement because the market value of mined coins is easier to ascertain than the production cost of global mining activities.

Mineable cryptocurrency could also be treated as a nonproduced asset in the sense that new coins are not truly created through mining. Rather, existing coins are discovered by providing mining services, a process that serves to ensure the value of the cryptocurrency and to introduce new coins into circulation. An illustrative example is a missing suitcase of money for which a finder's fee is offered; although the search efforts utilize capital and labor, the suitcase of money is not produced by rediscovering it. Therefore, even though cryptocurrency mining services involve activity that should fall within the production boundary, the discovered coins are not produced assets. In this scenario, cryptocurrencies are a new type of intangible asset like contracts or patents under nonproduced nonfinancial assets (OECD, 2018).

Any type of cryptocurrency may charge a fee for transactions in that currency. For mineable cryptocurrencies, this fee serves as an incentive for miners in addition to discovering new coins. For nonmineable cryptocurrencies, the transaction fee discourages a user from trading between their own digital addresses to artificially increase transaction volumes and thus inflate the price. The fee also rewards the validators, who operate servers that verify transactions through consensus on a blockchain network. In the balance of payments accounts, these transaction fees should be treated as exports of transaction verification services from the country in which the validator or miner resides and as an import of transaction verification services into the country where the payer resides (IMFSD, 2018).

Cryptocurrencies in trade accounting: practical considerations

Information available on the public ledger of most blockchains – like the amount, time and digital addresses of recipient and sender – is not always useful for balance of payments accounting purposes. When the owner of a digital address is anonymous, the country of residence for the sender and recipient and the purpose of the transaction are unknown. Thus attributing a cryptocurrency transaction to a specific country and categorizing it in international economic accounts are not possible without additional information.

Data collected by cryptocurrency exchanges and wallet providers may make it possible to identify the residency of the sender and the recipient for some transactions. For example, bank account or card information provided to exchanges may reveal country of residence, which could be used to estimate the stocks and flows of cryptocurrency between countries. Monitoring patterns in cryptocurrency transactions from information on the public blockchain could reveal the purpose of the payment for classification in international economic accounts. Cryptocurrency exchanges and wallets may be reluctant to share sensitive information about their customers, but statistical agencies may wish to contract with third-party data analysis companies to provide aggregated data for statistical purposes.

Another potential source of information is estimates from tax authorities on reported income from cryptocurrency. For example, cryptocurrency is treated as property for tax purposes in the United States, and users are required to report cryptocurrency-related income to the IRS. Two challenges of using tax data are that its use for non–tax purposes is often restricted and that cryptocurrency-related income may not be well reported.

Conclusion

Cryptocurrencies potentially remove barriers to making international transactions. As the industry develops, these financial instruments have the potential to facilitate even greater interconnectedness and globalization. Compared to transactions made using traditional payment methods, international cryptocurrency transactions typically incur lower fees and clear faster, while increasing trust and transparency between unrelated parties. But cryptocurrencies do not yet fully function as currencies due to their low acceptance and often volatile prices. International organizations are working with national statistical offices and central banks to develop guidelines for classifying cryptocurrency in national and international economic accounts. As the nature and use of cryptocurrency changes, these guidelines will evolve. The full impact of cryptocurrencies on international trade and transactions will be unknown until the cryptocurrency industry matures.

Note

1 The views expressed in this chapter are those of the author and do not necessarily represent those of the U.S. Bureau of Economic Analysis or the U.S. Department of Commerce.

References

Adrian, T., and Mancini-Griffoli, T. (2019). The rise of digital money. *Fin Tech Notes NOTE/19/01*, July 15, International Monetary Fund, Washington, DC. Retrieved from www.imf.org/~/media/Files/Publications/FTN063/2019/English/FTNEA2019001.ashx.

Blandin, A., Klein, K., Pieters, G., Rauchs, M., Recanatini, M., and Zhang, B. (2018). *2nd Global Cryptoasset Benchmarking Study*, December. Cambridge Centre for Alternative Finance, University of Cambridge Judge Business School. Retrieved from www.jbs.cam.ac.uk/fileadmin/user_upload/research/centres/alternative-finance/downloads/2018-12-ccaf-2nd-global-cryptoasset-benchmarking.pdf.

CoinMarketCap. (n.d.). Percentage of total market capitalization (dominance). Retrieved October 29, 2019 from https://coinmarketcap.com/charts.

Corbet, S., Lucey, B. M., Urquhart, A., and Yarovaya, L. (2019). Cryptocurrencies as a financial asset: A systematic analysis. *International Review of Financial Analysis*, 62, 182–199. https://doi.org/10.1016/j.irfa.2018.09.003.

Hileman, G. (2015). The Bitcoin market potential index. In M. Brenner, N. Christin, B. Johnson, and K. Rohloff (eds.), *Financial Cryptography and Data Security*. FC 2015. Lecture Notes in Computer Science (Vol. 8976). Berlin, Heidelberg: Springer. Retrieved from https://link.springer.com/chapter/10.1007/978-3-662-48051-9_7.

Hileman, G., and Rauchs, M. (2017). *2017 Global Cryptocurrency Benchmarking Study*. April 6. http://dx.doi.org/10.2139/ssrn.296543.

IMFSD (International Monetary Fund (IMF) Statistics Department). (2018). *Treatment of Crypto Assets in Macroeconomic Statistics*. BOPCOM 2018 Discussion Paper 18/11, October, International Monetary Fund, Washington, DC. Retrieved from www.imf.org/external/pubs/ft/bop/2018/pdf/18-11.pdf.

OECD (Organization for Economic Co-operation and Development), Working Party on Financial Statistics. (2018). *How to Deal with Bitcoin and Other Cryptocurrencies in the System of National Accounts?* Meeting of the Working Party on Financial Statistics 2018 Discussion Paper, October 29. Retrieved from www.oecd.org/officialdocuments/publicdisplaydocumentpdf/?cote=COM/SDD/DAF(2018)1&docLanguage=En.

Part III

Political and economic implications of cryptocurrencies

10 Central bank digital currency

Aims, mechanisms and macroeconomic impact

Silvia Dal Bianco

Introduction

According to the Bank of International Settlements, at least 40 central banks around the world are currently, or soon will be, researching and experimenting with Central Bank Digital Currency (CBDC) (Barontini and Holden, 2019). CBDC can have different attributes, such as, for example, being enabled by distributed ledger technlogy (DLT), being wholesale or general purpose. However, CBDC can be generally defined as some form of central bank money handled through electronic means and accessible to the broad public (Bindseil, 2020). To some extent, CBDC might resemble the functions and characteristics of cash. Hence it might act as an anonymous legal tender that allows fast intertemporal and international transactions at virtually zero cost, without the need of third trust parties, such as banks. Thus it is apparent that CBDC can have huge impact on the banking industry and on the economy as a whole.

The objective of this chapter is to employ the most up-to-date literature to shed light on the aims, working mechanisms and likely macroeconomic impact of CBDC.

The rest of the chapter is organized as follows. The second section describes and compares current payment systems to DLT-based ones. The third section explains the working mechanisms of CBDC, providing some real-world examples, and it discusses some of the potential benefits and macroeconomic risks associated with CBDC. Final remarks conclude.

Payment systems: state of the art versus DLT enabled

A payment system is a collection of technologies, laws and contracts that allow payments to occur and determine when a payment effects a settlement (Roberds, 2008). In the past decades, the volume of electronic payments processed by central banks' clearinghouses has been rising. On the one hand, this is due to the fact that banks' reserves accounts at central banks have been largely digitalized and, on the other, to the fact that many types of payment usually done with cash have gone electronic (Bech et al., 2018). As a result, the debate that started in the United States in the 1980s on whether the government should compete with the private sector in the provision of payment services, such as electronic funds, is extremely relevant nowadays (Congress, 1981). In particular, an increasing number of governments are looking to enter the payment systems' markets through the development of some sort of digital currency, possibly but not necessarily DLT enabled.

Nowadays, payment systems can be characterized as centralized, account based and tiered. First, centralization refers to the fact that the central bank sits at the center of the system. It represents the ultimate settlement agent, and it operates the real-time gross settlement (RTGS). For details on the European Union, see the European Central Bank: Payments and Securities (n.d.) Eurosystem; for the United States, see the Federal Reserve Board of Governors (n.d.) Payment Systems; for the UK, see the Bank of England Payment and Settlement (n.d.). Second, modern payment systems are account based. In order to have their payments settled, the acquirers of a good or service and the merchant do not directly interact with the central bank, but they engage in the payment system via their accounts at financial institutions, such as retail banks. Finally, payment systems are tiered. Financial institutions hold reserves at the central bank, which are used to settle payments with one another as a result of both direct interbank transactions or on behalf of their customers.

As noted by Greenspan (2008), one of the main shortcomings of the current payment systems is related to their centralization, which exposes financial markets and institutions to great vulnerability. For example, if a bad shock hits the ledgers at the Fed, the entire U.S. payment system would collapse. Another major problem is related to the lengthy payment settlement windows, which could be as long as three days.

DLT-enabled payment systems, such as the one of bitcoin, have the potential to overcome these difficulties. In particular, resembling at least in part the functioning of cash, they enable peer-to-peer transactions, without the need of a trusted intermediary, such as a bank, to validate and settle transactions (Nakamoto, 2008). More technically, this type of payment system is decentralized, as the control of the system is shared across the entire network, and distributed, as each network participant holds a copy of the ledger. Very importantly, the validity of a transaction depends on the network users' trust in the consensus reached among themselves. In the case of bitcoin, the validating mechanism is called proof of work (PoW) (for more details, see Böhme et al., 2015).

Not surprisingly, DLT-based payment systems have some potential benefits, and they also present some challenging aspects. On the positive side, as noticed by Batlin et al. (2016), bitcoin blockchain could enable near real-time settlement. Then, international money transfers can be made more cost-effective, the fees associated with the transfer of bitcoin being much lower than the ones for remittances (World Bank, 2019). Further, thanks to cryptography, network users can both validate their identity while protecting their privacy. Finally, being distributed, it is virtually impossible to destroy every copy of the ledger, and thus the payment system should be more resilient to malicious attacks. On the negative side, the potential challenges are related to the protocol's consensus mechanism, scalability and costs. Bitcoin is a decentralized digital payment system whose viability crucially depends on upon the mitigation of the so-called double-spending and Byzantine generals' problems through the PoW-based consensus (for full details, see Dourado and Brito, 2014). Chiu and Koeppl (2018) model the PoW as a Cournot game and find that a cryptocurrency is less prone to double-spending attacks when the individual transaction size is small relative to the overall volume of transactions, like in a classical payment system. Further, Biais et al. (2019a, 2019b) show that in permissionless blockchains, multiple equilibria can exist. Hence, the longest chain without forking is just one of the possible stable outcomes of the bitcoin protocol. Thus the overall system appears quite "fragile." Turning to costs, they are related to electricity consumption and transaction fees (for further details, see Lipton, 2018). Finally, a further fundamental issue is related to the so-called scalability, i.e., the relative limited transaction volume and verification speed of the system. For example, while the bitcoin blockchain can only process seven transactions per second, Visa can process up to 65,000 transactions per second, using less than 0.5 percent of bitcoin's electricity consumption.

In conclusion, as remarked by the European Central Bank and Bank of Japan with project Stella (European Central Bank and Bank of Japan, 2017), there are reasons for being optimistic, but DLT technology still appears immature for operating central banks' payment systems.

Central Banks Digital Currency (CBDC): design, implementation and macroeconomic impact

In the definition of Bordo and Levin (2017), digital currency is "an asset stored in electronic form that can serve essentially the same function as physical currency, namely facilitating payments transactions." More specifically, central banks are now debating the opportunity of introducing CBDC. According to the so-called BIS money flower (Bank for International Settlements, 2018), CBDC can be either token or account based as well as for general or wholesale purposes. For the concerns of "token-based" digital currencies, they rely critically on the ability of the payee to verify the validity of the payment object. According to Cœuré (2018), this type of digital currencies will be based on a DLT or comparable cryptographic technology. Account-based digital currencies, instead, depend fundamentally on the ability to verify the identity of the account holder. Then CBDC could be primarily targeted at retail transactions (i.e., so-called general purposes CBDC), or it could be designed for wholesale payment and settlement transactions, such as interbank payments (i.e., wholesale CBDC).

The World Economic Forum (2019) white paper shows that the majority of central banks are devoting their research and experimenting efforts to token-based retail CDBCs and to account-based wholesale CDBCs.

In essence, token-based retail CBDCs are meant to be the digital version of cash. Hence, the general public would be granted direct access to central banks' liabilities. According to Meaning et al. (2018), such an "electronic, fiat liability of a central bank" would fulfill all the economic functions of money. However, as brilliantly stated by Mike Orcutt (2020), "[C]ash is a paradox," i.e., a very old technology that has proved to be not replicable in a more modern form. DLT technology can enable retail CBDC, although the trade-off generated by anonymity, scalability and availability have not been fully assessed.

Further, echoing the idea of Tobin (1987), CBDC would also allow consumers and businesses to hold accounts at the central banks much like the ones currently held by banks. With the aim of boosting financial inclusion, the possibility of "central bank deposited currency accounts" has been experimented with in Ecuador, through Dinero Electrónico. This project, which does not use DLT, was suspended after three years, and it has received mixed reviews (see Moncayo Lara & Reis, 2019; Campuzano Vásquez et al., 2018). Another interesting case is provided by the e-krona, the CBDC of the Swedish Central Bank, i.e., Riksbank (for details, see Sveriges Riksbank, 2020). The pilot project started in February 2020 and it is due to last one year. The pilot is structured in two tiers. In the first tier, the Riksbank issues e-kronor to participants in an e-krona network, such as banks. In the second tier, participants distribute e-kronor to end users. It is not known whether DLT has been employed. Even so, the e-krona ecosystem seems to resemble the state-of-the-art payment system, insofar as banks still hold end users' accounts.

Parallel to the central banks' projects and pilots, a number of scholars have started to investigate the impact of CBDC on economic growth and monetary policy. Using a DSGE model paired with quarterly U.S. data for 1990–2006, Barrdear and Kumhof (2016) find that an injection of CBDC stimulates long-run economic growth and that it can also help stabilize business cycles and financial systems. Niepelt (2018) takes a different angle and shows that the introduction of CBDC similar to central bank–deposited currency accounts or "reserves for all" can have macroeconomic effects that are not necessarily adverse. However, CBDC skeptics argue that deposit accounts at the central bank would increase not only the risk of structural disintermediation of banks and centralization of the credit allocation process within the central bank but also the risk of facilitation systemic runs on banks in crisis situations (for an up-to-date review, see Bindseil, 2020).

Turning to monetary policy, CBDCs' effects on policy rates largely depend on CBDC design. For example, Dyson and Hodgson (2016) argue for nonremunerating central bank–deposited currency accounts. The reason is twofold. On the one hand, this might pose governments under financial strain. On the other, the "new" policy rate would serve to remunerate deposits at the central bank and not to influence the borrowing cost of central bank reserves. Hence, the bank rate would be a very different policy tool with potentially unpredictable impact. However, according to Bindseil (2014), introducing CBDC can strengthen the transmission mechanism for three reasons: (1) it allows overcoming the zero lower bound (ZLB), as negative interest rates can be applied to

CBDC;. (2) interest rates on CBDC provide for additional monetary policy instruments, independently of ZLB; and (3) CBDC can facilitate the ability to provide helicopter money.

Conclusions

The present chapter has shown that the debate surrounding the design, implementation and macroeconomic effects of CBDC is extremely lively. In particular, no firm conclusion about the potential of alternative payment systems and of CBDC has been reached. This is partially due to the fact that central banks' projects in the field are relatively recent and not always clearly communicated (World Economic Forum, 2019). Actually, not hearing more about CBDC during the 2020 pandemic crisis is quite surprising.

Couldn't CBDC provide fresh resources to businesses and households in difficulty? Wouldn't CBDC cut bureaucracy and lengthy applications for loans? Shouldn't coordinated monetary and fiscal policies be preferred to uncoordinated ones?

These questions are left to wait, patiently, for future research.

References

Bank for International Settlements. (2018). *Central Bank Digital Currencies*. Online Edition. Retrieved August 24, 2020, from www.bis.org.

Bank of England Payment and Settlement. (n.d.). Retrieved from www.bankofengland. co.uk/payment-and-settlement.

Barontini, C., and Holden, H. (2019). *Proceeding with Caution – a Survey on Central Bank Digital Currency*. BIS Paper 101.

Barrdear, J., and Kumhof, M. (2016). *The Macroeconomics of Central Bank Issued Digital Currencies*. Bank of England, Staff Working Paper No. 605 currencies. (605).

Batlin, A., Hyder, J., Murphy, C., Przewloka, A., and Williams, S. (2016). *Building the Trust Engine: How the Blockchain Could Transform Finance (and the World) A UBS Group Technology White Paper*. Retrieved August 24, 2020, from https://www.ubs.com/microsites/ blockchain-report/en/home.html.

Bech, M. L., Faruqui, U., Ougaard, F., and Picillo, C. (2018). Payments are A-Changin' but cash still rules. *BIS Quarterly Review*, March 11. Retrieved from SSRN: https://ssrn.com/ abstract=3139217.

Biais, B., Bisière, C., Bouvard, M., and Casamatta, C. (2019a). The blockchain folk theorem. *The Review of Financial Studies*, 32 (5), 1662–1715. https://doi.org/10.1093/rfs/ hhy095.

Biais, B., Bisière, C., Bouvard, M., and Casamatta, C. (2019b). Blockchains, coordination, and forks. *AEA Papers and Proceedings*, 109, 88–92.

Bindseil, U. (2014). *Monetary Policy Operations and the Financial System*. Oxford: Oxford University Press.

Bindseil, U. (2020). *Tiered CBDC and the Financial System*. Working Paper Series 2351, European Central Bank.

Böhme, R., Christin, N., Edelman, B., and Moore, T. (2015). Bitcoin: Economics, technology, and governance. *Journal of Economic Perspectives*, 29 (2), 213–238.

Bordo, M., and Levin, A. T. (2017). *Central Bank Digital Currency and the Future of Monetary Policy*. Economics Working Papers 17104, Hoover Institution, Stanford University.

Campuzano Vásquez, J. A., Chávez Cruz, G. Jr., y Maza Iñiguez, J. (2018). El fracaso del dinero electrónico en Ecuador. *3C Empresa: Investigación y pensamiento crítico*, 7 (3), 82–101.

Chiu, J., and Koeppl, T. V. (2018). *Incentive Compatibility on the Blockchain*. May. Retrieved from SSRN: https://ssrn.com/abstract=3221233 or http://dx.doi.org/10.2139/ssrn.3221233.

Cœuré, B. (2018). *The Future of Central Bank Money*. Geneva: International Center for Monetary and Banking Studies, May 14.

Congress. (1981). *Should the Federal Reserve Offer Electronic Funds Transfer Services?* Hearing before a Subcommittee of the Committee on Government Operations, House of Representatives, Ninety-Seventh Congress, October 22, First Session.

Dourado, E., and Brito, J. (2014). Cryptocurrency. In Steven N. Durlauf and Lawrence E. Blume (eds.), *The New Palgrave Dictionary of Economics*. Online Edition. Retrieved from https://www.mercatus.org/system/files/cryptocurrency-article.pdf.

Dyson, B., and Hodgson, G. (2016). *Digital Cash: Why Central Banks Should Start Issuing Electronic Money*. Technical report, Positive Money.

European Central Bank: Payments and Securities. (n.d.). Retrieved from www.ecb.europa.eu/ecb/tasks/paym/html/index.en.html.

European Central Bank and Bank of Japan. (2017). *Project Stella – Payment Systems: Liquidity Saving Mechanisms in a Distributed Ledger Environment*. Retrieved from www.ecb.europa.eu/pub/pdf/other/ecb.stella_project_report_september_2017.pdf.

Federal Reserve Board of Governors. (n.d.). *Payment Systems*. Retrieved from www.federalreserve.gov/paymentsystems.htm.

Greenspan, A. (2008). *The Age of Turbulence: Adventures in a New World*. New York: Penguin.

Lipton, A. (2018). Blockchains and distributed ledgers in retrospective and perspective. *High-Performance Computing in Finance: Problems, Methods, and Solutions*, 537–560.

Meaning, J., Dyson, B., Barker, J., and Clayton, E. (2018). *Broadening Narrow Money: Monetary Policy with a Central Bank Digital Currency*. Bank of England Working Paper No. 724.

Moncayo Lara, J., and Reis, M. (2019). Un Análisis Inicial del Dinero Electrónico en Ecuador y su Impacto en la Inclusión Financiera. *Cuestiones Económicas*, 25 (1).

Nakamoto, S. (2008). *Bitcoin: A Peer-to-Peer Electronic Cash System*. Retrieved from https://bitcoin.org/bitcoin.pdf.

Niepelt, D. (2018). *Reserves for All? Central Bank Digital Currency, Deposits, and Their (Non)-Equivalence*. CEPR Discussion Paper Series, DP13065(July).

Orcutt, M. (2020). An elegy for cash: The technology we might never replace. *MIT Technology Review*, January 3.

Roberds, W. (2008). *Payment Systems the New Palgrave Dictionary of Economics*. 2nd Edition. Edited by Steven N. Durlauf and Lawrence E. Blume. London: Palgrave Macmillan.

Sveriges Riksbank. (2020). *The Riksbank's E-Krona Pilot*. Reg. no 2019–00291.

Tobin, J. (1987). The case for preserving regulatory distinctions. In *Proceedings of the Economic Policy Symposium* (pp. 167–183). Jackson Hole: Federal Reserve Bank of Kansas City.

World Bank. (2019). *Remittance Prices Worldwide*. Issue 30, June. Retrieved from https://remittanceprices.worldbank.org/sites/default/files/rpw_annex_q2_2019.pdf.

World Economic Forum. (2019). *Central Banks and Distributed Ledger Technology: How are Central Banks Exploring Blockchain Today?* White paper. Retrieved from www.weforum.org/whitepapers/central-banks-and-distributed-ledger-technology-how-are-central-banks-exploring-blockchain-today.

11 Crypto money and cryptocurrency competition

Björn Holste and Thomas Mayer

From commodity money to credit money

To give an account of crypto money and its role in currency competition, we begin with a recap of the historic development of monetary systems and their key features. Eucken (1989) identifies three types of the monetary system:

1   The *commodity money* system, where a good becomes a means of exchange.
2   The *debt money* system, where a means of exchange is created as debt when a good is delivered or a service provided.
3   The *credit money* system, where a means of exchange is created via credit extension.

Eucken finds that past and current monetary orders have all been combinations of systems, albeit with different weights in the various orders.

Since 1971, when Richard Nixon cut the link of the USD to gold, we live in a pure credit money system. Banks create money for the borrowers through a simple balance sheet extension: credit is entered on the asset side of the balance sheet as a claim on the borrower, and money is entered on the liability side as debt to the borrower. When borrowers transfer their money to another bank, the bank sending the money needs to borrow it back from the bank receiving it. Since there are more than two banks in any given system, a market for interbank loans emerges. When there are many banks, the market needs a clearing house. And when the clearing house not only matches the supply and demand of interbank credit but also acts as a lender and depositor to clear the market, it becomes a central bank. By standing ready to lend to banks or to take deposits from them at preannounced rates, the central bank steers the rate in the money market and, indirectly through this, the rates in the credit market.

Unlike in the gold standard, there is no natural anchor to money creation through credit extension by banks. Theoretically, banks could extend their balance sheet as far as they like. But the quality of money would deteriorate if there is no restriction. Moreover, any loss of credit would destroy a corresponding amount of money, inducing a shortage of money and possibly deflation. To secure the quality of money and to protect the money stock, the state requires banks to set aside a certain amount of equity when they increase credit. Thus, credit extension is constrained by banks' ability to create or attract equity, and money is protected by a first loss insurance in the form of banks' equity cushion. However, as credit losses could also affect the whole banking system and exceed total bank equity, the state provides insurance of money against credit losses beyond the coverage through first loss insurance. In view of the pivotal roles of banks, the central bank and the state, we can describe the existing credit money system as a public–private partnership for money production.

Money, economic stability and growth: Hayek versus Keynes

Mainstream economics today is dominated by the New Keynesian Model, which has neither a banking sector nor a capital market. Money enters the model "exogenously" (i.e., drops from heaven), and investment is assumed always to be identical to savings. Hence, the ability of banks to create new money for investors without having to collect existing money savings is disregarded. Moreover, since the model does not recognize that capital needs first to be produced before it can be used and that capital production takes time, it fails to capture the ability of banks to create credit and investment boom-bust cycles over time. Hence, mainstream economists did not foresee the Great Financial Crisis of 2007/2008.

In this crisis, the credit money system needed to be stabilized by central banks, and money needed to be reinsured by states. As a result, the role of the credit money system for the emergence of credit and investment cycles, which had been missed by mainstream economics, has received renewed attention. Based on the work of Knut Wicksell, Ludwig von Mises and Friedrich von Hayek, an increasing number of financial analysts and economists have identified the creation of money through credit extension by commercial banks under the guidance of central banks as a source of economic instability.[1] When a central bank manages interest rates in the credit markets below the "natural rate" (at which money savings and investments are in equilibrium), more money is created through credit extension for new investment while money savings are discouraged. A credit and investment boom ensues, during which investment temporarily exceeds saving. When capacity constraints put a brake on the investment expansion, prices rise, prompting the central bank to induce an increase in credit market rates. Higher interest rates discourage new investment and render some investment undertaken at lower rates economically unviable. As bank loans need to be written off and new investment drops, the boom turns into bust. Credit and investment boom-bust cycles would, of course, be avoided, if the central bank could stabilize the credit market rate at the level of the natural rate. But as this rate is unobservable, the central bank engages in a process of trial and error to find the correct level for the credit market rate, inducing boom-bust cycles in the process.[2]

As a consequence, a number of economists and analysts have proposed to replace money creation through bank credit extension by direct money issuance by the central bank or a private entity or by linking money to an existing asset.[3] It was deep disappointment about the credit money system that induced Satoshi Nakamoto, at the peak of the Great Financial Crisis of 2007/2008, to propose bitcoin as money in the form of an asset instead of a liability (Nakamoto, 2008).

From payment tokens to asset tokens

The old concept of blockchain technology as a cryptographically sealed database with special properties (Gifford, 1982), which was revived by the failings of the credit money system in the financial crisis, made it possible to create virtual commodity money. The first generation of pure "payment tokens," to which bitcoin belongs, was followed by further generations of "tokens" up to today's most advanced "asset tokens," which open up a new perspective for the generation of money. Table 11.1 gives an overview of the most important existing and possible forms of money today.

The demand for the various forms of money is likely to depend on the stability of purchasing power, security as a means of preserving value, ease of use, transaction costs and market penetration. Bitcoin has numerous of advantages over credit money. Since money is no longer created as a liability through lending, its regulation, insurance and administration require neither a state nor a central bank. The security of transactions and value retention is ensured by

Table 11.1 Forms of money

Type of money	Description	Profit from the creation of money (Seigniorage)
Credit money	Created as a private bank liability through lending	Positive, as long as the interest on the loan exceeds the interest on the liabilities
Central bank money	Banknotes or tokens issued by a central bank as a nonrepayable obligation and covered only indirectly by assets	Positive, as long as the interest on assets exceeds the interest on liabilities
Private payment token	Uncovered electronic scrip issued by a company or network	Positive, as long as the increase in the token offer exceeds the costs for token issuance and processing of payment transactions
Asset token	Issued as a claim on assets and exchangeable into these assets	Positive or negative, depending on whether the return on assets exceeds or falls short of the cost of issuing tokens and validating transactions

blockchain technology, which also simplifies and expedites the execution of transactions. The transaction costs are financed by seigniorage, which goes to computer operators (called miners) as remuneration for proving the validity of transactions in the blockchain.

Disadvantages are that the purchasing power of bitcoin and other payment tokens depends solely on supply and demand. As long as the market penetration is low and the legal tender remains the predominant unit for pricing goods and of account, the purchasing power of the payment tokens fluctuates enormously. In addition, the cost of transactions in the bitcoin blockchain has increased over time because of increased mathematical complexity of the validation of transactions. For the same reason, the speed of processing in the classic bitcoin blockchain has decreased.

The ability to integrate smart contracts into blockchains has opened the door to the issuance of asset tokens. These tokens constitute a contractual right to another value and are therefore traded at the price of this value. Their purchasing power is thus as stable as the value to which they are linked and as the credibility of this link. Their market penetration does not depend primarily on the supply and demand for the tokens but on the supply and demand for the underlying assets. In view of the higher purchasing power stability and the associated market penetration, these tokens are also referred to as "stable coins." In order to reduce costs and increase the speed of transaction validation, issuers may also use a "permissioned" blockchain, where only a limited number of authorized entities are permitted to participate in the validation. Whether users will have to bear the cost of transactions arising from the need to validate the transaction in the blockchain depends on whether the underlying assets yield returns. If so, the issuer of the token may use the returns to finance transaction costs and offer users' payments with the tokens free of charge. If this is not the case, the issuer must charge the users for the transaction costs.

From asset tokens to Libra

Libra is designed as "a stable currency based on a secure and stable open source blockchain, backed by assets and managed by an independent association" (Libra Association, 2019). A basket of existing credit money currencies created by central and commercial banks that are internationally convertible, liquid and stable in purchasing power serves as cover stock. Thus Libra is a cryptocurrency based on credit money. The Libra money supply grows with the purchases of the users, who use conventional money for it.

Libra could become attractive for future users because it offers instant, cost-effective, peer-to-peer money transfers at any size and over any distance and a stable instrument for the preservation of value with low risks from exchange rate fluctuations of the reserve basket against third currencies. It could also become a unit of account if suppliers on global trading platforms decide to price their goods in Libra. Considering that Facebook and its subsidiaries today have around 2.7 billion users and that future association members will add more potential users, Libra's customer potential is well above that of any exist-ing currency.

Probably because of this, Libra has met strong resistance especially from three groups who all have an interest to preserve the credit money system in its present form. Commercial banks fear that they will lose customers if Libra becomes the preferred instrument for transactions. Central banks fear that their ability to steer the economy will diminish if a substantial part of the outstand-ing money is covered by short-term government loans. And politicians fear that they will become dependent on a large borrower to finance government spending who is only interested in short-term Treasury bills. We would add a further objection: as it is based on credit money, Libra would not eliminate the financial and economic instability, which Hayek and others have criticized and which Nakomoto has referred to as a motivation for the development of bitcoin.

Digital central bank money

As the going monetary order evolved from having a core of commodity money to a credit money system, the central banks became ever more powerful. In the wake of the Great Financial Crisis, they became the indispensable power in economics and politics or, as the central bankers phrased it, "the only game in town." Since central bankers have a natural aversion against money systems that can do without them, they have fiercely opposed cryptocurrencies. However, the launch of the Libra project has raised doubts among them as to whether they will be able to suppress these currencies forever. Hence, central bankers have begun to think about digital central bank currencies as challengers to private cryptocurrencies.

Digital central bank currencies can be designed as add-ons to the existing credit money or as a replacement for credit money with transfers recorded in a central or distributed ledger (Bindseil, 2020). In our view, there is a strong case for a digital central bank currency based on distributed ledger technology to replace credit money in the European Monetary Union. Digitization of the euro (in this way) would not only increase the competitiveness of the euro against other private and public cryptocurrencies but also put the common European currency on a more stable base (Mayer, 2019). The first step toward such a digital euro would be to introduce a bank deposit fully backed with central bank money. The European Central Bank (ECB) could create the cen-tral bank money necessary for covering the deposit by purchasing government bonds. In a second step, the secure deposit could be set up as digital central bank money that can be transferred peer-to-peer using blockchain technology. Like other "stable coins," the euro would become an "asset token," backed solely by government bonds. Only the ECB (and not the commercial banks as in the credit money system) would be responsible for issuing it. To protect it from abuse by governments and counterfeiting, it could be endowed with a digital watermark by embedding the rules for the original establishment and future increase of money supply as a "smart contract" in the asset token.

Money supply would be increased by further purchases of government bonds, but these purchases would have to be decided independently of political influence and from a long-term perspective. For instance, growth of the digital euro money supply could be geared to the expected growth potential of the euro area economy. Instead of through bank lending, money supply would be expanded by increasing ECB holdings of government bonds. To avoid monetary financing of budget deficits (as proposed by Modern Monetary Theory), governments could commit themselves to distribute the money they receive from the bond sales directly to their citizens as a "money dividend."

Commercial banks would now have to broker their customers' savings deposits in the form of digital euros to investors. They could, of course, continue to create private debt money through lending, but there would be no state guarantee for conversion at parity into digital euros. Thus banks would resemble investment funds whose assets are protected against first loss by an equity cushion. Savers could choose the bank that suits them according to their preferences for returns and first loss protection. The central bank would no longer manipulate interest rates to manage banks' credit money creation for policy purposes. But in view of the new impotence of monetary policy, this would hardly matter.

Digitization offers the possibility of a "new deal" to reduce the outstanding debt of the euro states in the market and to safeguard the euro: the fiscally conservative northern countries would agree to the one-off monetization of old debt on the balance sheet of the ECB for the creation of secure money. In return, the highly indebted southern countries would accept that after the one-off monetization of their old debts, bailouts through debt monetization would be impossible in the future. As government bonds in the amount of about 7 trillion euros would be taken out of the market to back the money stock, the public debt of all euro area countries could be reduced to less than 25 percent of GDP. This would give every one of them new room for prudent fiscal policy.

Money created through bank credit needs a state for its reinsurance that cannot be built for the euro area. Digital money, on the other hand, can exist without a state guarantee. A digital euro issued by the ECB would not only be unbreakable but could also prove its quality as a global means of transaction and store of value in competition with other domestic and foreign digital and credit currencies.

Conclusion

When paper money came from China to Europe in the seventeenth century, it was initially issued by private entities in competition with one another. However, fractional reserve banking created risks for paper money holders (as banknotes were only partly backed by the assets that they were supposed to represent), and as these risks materialized, states and central banks assumed important roles in managing and guarding money creation. Cryptocurrencies can tie up to the history of paper money and avoid its fate of being taken over by states as long as their supply is not increased through fractional reserve banking. Like the early versions of paper money, they can be issued both privately and publicly and compete with one another to offer the user the optimal utility from the use of money (Hayek, 1976). State monopolies operate very rarely in the best interest of consumers. Money issuance is no exception.

Notes

1 For a comprehensive exposition of the theory, see Huerta de Soto (2012) and Mayer (2018).
2 The search for the "correct" rate is described in the Taylor Rule, which explains actual central bank policy relatively well.
3 An early proposal for direct money issuance by the central bank was the Chicago Plan of 1933, explained in Fisher (1935). A more recent project of direct money issuance by a private entity is bitcoin, described in Nakamoto (2008). For a proposal to back money fully with gold, see, e.g., Huerta de Soto (2012).

References

Bindseil, U. (2020). *Tiered CBDC and the Financial System.* ECB Working Paper Series, No 2351 / January.

Eucken, W. (1989). *Die Grundlagen der Nationalökonomie.* Berlin: Springer.

Fisher, I. (1935). *100% Money.* New Haven: The City.

Gifford, David K. (1982). Cryptographic sealing for information secrecy and authentication. *Communications of the ACM*, 25 (4), April, 274–286. New York: ACM.

Hayek, F. A. (1976). *Denationalisation of Money.* London: The Institute of Economic Affairs.

Huerta de Soto, J. (2012). *Money, Bank Credit, and Economic Cycles.* Auburn, AL: Ludwig von Mises Institute.

Libra Association. (2019). *White Paper.* Retrieved from https://libra.org/en-US/white-paper/#the-libra-blockchain.

Mayer, T. (2018). *Austrian Economics, Money and Finance.* Oxon and New York: Routledge.

Mayer, T. (2019). *A Digital Euro to Save EMU.* Retrieved from www.voxeu.org.

Nakamoto, S. (2008). *Bitcoin: A Peer-to-Peer Electronic Cash System.* Retrieved from https://bitcoin.org/bitcoin.pdf.

12 The geoeconomics of cryptocurrencies

An institutional perspective

Andrew Isaak, Suleika Bort and Michael Woywode

Introduction

The value of money as reflected in exchange rates (Pigou, 1917) has been shown to be highly volatile, such as during the global financial crisis of 2008. This crisis illustrated that political instability, technological progress and negative future expectations of a country's economic development can lead to a loss of trust in national currencies and the financial system as a whole (e.g., Stix, 2013). In this situation, a person behind the pseudonym "Satoshi Nakamoto" devised a white paper describing a new currency called bitcoin that was independent of institutions such as banks, central banks and investment companies and that was more direct, faster and more transparent than traditional currency systems (Nakamoto, 2008). This bitcoin system relies upon a decentralized network to verify all transactions via a public ledger (i.e., the blockchain). Bitcoins are not directly backed by a government or a central bank and are therefore truly decentralized (Weber, 2014). Bitcoin circulation is limited to 21 million, which are successively mined by performing complex calculations. The underlying price of a bitcoin is based on the cost involved in mining the coins as well as on this artificial supply shortage. While a growing number of cryptocurrencies exist, the bitcoin algorithm remains a dominant design in this new market (Geroski, 2003).

For several years, bitcoins were primarily for the technically inclined. However, due to rapid growth, bitcoin market capitalization reached approximately USD 131,087,151,088 (131 billion), commanding 67 percent of the total cryptocurrency market[1] and surpassing the narrow stock of money of countries such as the United Kingdom and Portugal at the end of the year 2019.[2] Figure 12.1 illustrates the dramatic increase in bitcoin market capitalization from 2016 through 2019.

Several countries have recently issued their own cryptocurrencies (e.g., Ecuador, Senegal, Singapore, Tunisia and Venezuela) with others in the late exploration phase (e.g., China, Estonia, Japan, Palestine, Russia and Sweden).[3] Further, the first bitcoin exchange-traded fund (ETF) received regulatory approval across the European Union.

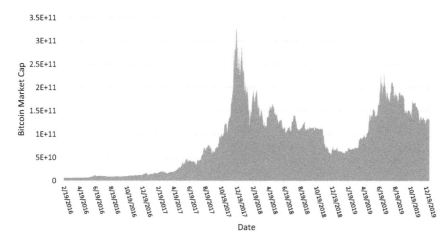

Figure 12.1 Bitcoin market capitalization, 2016–2019

Source: https://coin.dance/stats/marketcaphistorical

Yet for any currency to prevail and have value, trust is an absolute requirement. Like fiat money, bitcoins have no intrinsic value (Cheah & Fry, 2015). In contrast to fiat money, the value of bitcoins is not connected to a government or state but is derived only from a critical mass of users that accept bitcoins in exchange for commodities or services (e.g., Bjerg, 2016, p. 61). In such a regulation-free market with a largely anonymous trading mechanism, corruption may be an issue since such situations are attractive to those laundering money from drugs and other illegal sources. Changing economic and regulatory conditions have impacted the attractiveness of bitcoin trading in various countries. While some nations such as Japan legalized bitcoin trading and even declared it as a currency, in other markets such as China drastic measures were taken to forbid trading entirely. Figure 12.2 depicts mean bitcoin trading volume by country in our sample with a 95 percent confidence interval.

Overall, the bitcoin trading market is characterized not only by strong variation in trading volume across countries but also by stark differences in degrees of regulation. These contrasting institutional environments have different effects on the growth and development paths of bitcoins and on cryptocurrencies in general, which this chapter aims to explore – entailing the theoretical background, data, methodology, results and discussion.

Institutions and new market emergence

Institutions provide the "rules of the game" and designate "humanly devised constraints that structure human interaction" (North, 1990, p. 3). According

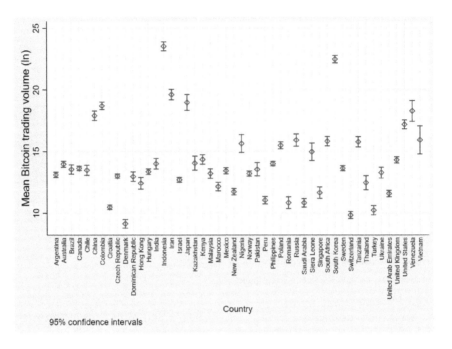

Figure 12.2 Mean bitcoin trading volume by country

to North (1990), institutions have informal aspects (e.g., cultural values and norms), as well as formal components (e.g., rules, regulations and laws), both of which govern firm behavior. Scott (1995) further classified these aspects of institutions into three pillars: regulative, normative and cultural-cognitive. These pillars help explain how new organizational forms gain and maintain legitimacy by conforming to the rules and norms of the institutional environment (Dimaggio & Powell, 1983; Meyer & Rowan, 1977) and therefore serve as an important framework for examining how new markets emerge and develop (e.g., Stephan et al., 2015).

Corruption and the emergence and development of bitcoin trading

Kaufmann et al. (2010, p. 3) define corruption as "the extent to which public power is exercised for private gain," which includes such activities as bribery, nepotism, patronage and embezzlement. Most research examining the relationship between corruption and conducting business focuses on the increase in costs associated with corrupt practices – i.e., whether or not an entrepreneur gets involved in corrupt activities (e.g., Becker, 1968). A high level of corruption in a country creates market and resource allocation inefficiencies, increasing the costs of production and management (Cuervo-Cazurra, 2006), deterring foreign direct investment (Habib & Zurawicki, 2002; Wei, 2000) and reducing entrepreneurs' growth aspirations (Estrin et al., 2013).

According to Tanzi (1995, p. 24), four factors in particular determine the degree to which corruption plays a part in a country: (1) the role of the state and the range of instruments it uses, (2) social characteristics of a society (e.g., the extent to which arm's-length relationships prevail), (3) the political system in place and (4) the sanctioning (penalty) system for uncovered acts of corruption.

Prior research suggests that if entrepreneurs assume that the societal acceptance of corruption is low, the legal (and political) framework is strong, restrictions are high and both are enforced (e.g., credible sanction threats versus cheap talk), they will be less likely to be involved in illegal activities and vice versa (e.g., Andersson, 2003). At the same time, ethnographic studies show that talented illegal entrepreneurs are not necessarily successful in legitimate business domains, as they struggle to cope with the formal requirements of a legal enterprise (Adler, 1993). Therefore, while illegal activities and corruption are costly, it is also conceivable that corruption may grease the wheels of overly restrictive economies or those with preexisting bad business climates that create high government burdens for start-ups.

Since the origins of bitcoins remain clouded in uncertainty, they are often classified as nonlegal currency and have been accused of supporting illegal transactions.[4] For example, early bitcoin adopters were Internet marketplaces that valued greater anonymity and the absence of rules concerning what could be bought or sold (e.g., gambling or online drug sales; see Böhme et al., 2015). Christin (2013) found that transaction volume grew sharply when these marketplaces introduced bitcoin. Finally, bitcoins have been used to evade international capital controls such as those in China or Argentina (Punwasi, 2017). In April 2018, Interpol initiated a Working Group on Cryptocurrencies and the Darknet.[5] Yet, to date, no central monitoring body exists for cryptocurrencies.

Clearly, social norms play a large role here (e.g., Goudie & Stasavage, 1998). If corruption in a country is perceived as commonplace and lighter types of corruption such as tax evasion or small bribes to facilitate business transactions are perceived as typical or as only a minor transgression with few or no social sanctions, we would expect this to impact the respective level of bitcoin trading in the given country:

> *H1: A higher level of corruption perception in a country is positively related to bitcoin trading.*

Voice, information asymmetry and efficient markets

An efficient market is one in which all market participants have all the information available and where the asset prices reflect all available information

(Malkiel & Fama, 1970). In contrast, information asymmetry refers to situations where some economic agents have more information than others (Akerlof, 1970). Greater freedom of expression and freedom of association (i.e., voice) in a given country reduce information asymmetry between firms and investors, leading to better informed decision makers and thus to a more efficient market. Prior research confirms that the governance environment strongly impacts on investment mode choice (Li & Filer, 2007) since a free press, freedom of expression, as well as the accountability of public officials are necessary preconditions to reporting misconduct such as insider trading (e.g., US Supreme Court, 1987). The more information available on the market, the more it approaches an ideal information landscape that matches investors with firms, reducing moral hazard (Jensen & Meckling, 1976), i.e., situations where one party exploits their superior knowledge of the risk of an asset or transaction at the expense of another. Thus, we expect that when there are well functioning classical investment vehicles (such as stock and bond markets), there is less need for average investors to explore alternative investments such as cryptocurrency in order to earn solid returns at a given level of risk. Simultaneously, the media plays a crucial role for investors in gauging the risk-return ratio of investment assets (e.g., Bhattacharya et al., 2009). Hence, a higher voice should also lead to a higher awareness among investors of the risks of particularly speculative investments. For example, in Russia the media serves a crucial role in creating awareness of malpractice and investment risks (Dyck et al., 2008). Thus, we assume:

> *H2: A higher voice and accountability perception in a country is negatively related to bitcoin trading.*

Data and sample

We rely on a data set that is part of a larger research project on institutions and cryptocurrencies (Isaak & Bort, 2019). To test our hypotheses, we use longitudinal data on weekly bitcoin trading volume for 2010–2018 in 48 countries with unique currencies compiled using the tables of the 109 unique platforms listed on bitcoin charts.[6]

Measures

Dependent variable

Bitcoin trading volume

Our dependent variable is the weekly trading volume in USD in each country. Since our dependent variable is highly skewed (skewness: 38.03), we used the natural logarithm to account for this distribution.

Independent variables

Corruption

We use the Corruption Perception Index (CPI) provided annually by Transparency International since 1995.[7] It relies on the informed views of analysts, businesspeople and experts worldwide, e.g., expert assessment and opinion surveys, reported for 176 countries.[8] A higher score means citizens perceive their country to have less corruption. To ease interpretation, we reversed the coding of this variable so that higher scores mean more corruption. This variable is highly correlated ($r = 0.995$) with the control of corruption dimension of the six-dimensional[9] governance index of the Worldwide Governance Indicators (WGI) available via the World Bank[10] (Kaufmann et al., 2010). The CPI variable is also highly positively correlated ($r = 0.891$) with the GDP per capita (in current USD) defined as the gross domestic product divided by mid-year population.[11]

Voice and accountability

We used the voice and accountability dimension of the composite measure of six dimensions of the Worldwide Governance Indicators (WGI) as calculated by Kaufmann et al. (2010).[12] The voice and accountability index of the World Bank is a perceptive measure of freedom of expression, freedom of association, a free media and the degree to which citizens can select their government in a given country.[13]

Control variables

Interest rate

We controlled for the financial context in a particular country via the real interest rate measured by the lending interest rate adjusted for inflation as measured by the GDP deflator.[14]

Google bitcoin attention

We also controlled for bitcoin search attention by country as an indicator of public interest in bitcoins.[15] Prior research acknowledges the importance of media coverage for the emergence of new industries (e.g., Sine et al., 2005). Google Trends has been used in finance to quantify new Internet phenomena (Kristoufek, 2013; Cheah & Fry, 2015). Thus Kristoufek (2013) found a strong positive correlation between bitcoin prices and corresponding search terms. We used the natural logarithm to account for the variable distribution.

Number of alternative cryptocurrencies

We counted the number of alternative cryptocurrencies active per year (e.g., Ethereum), studying press releases and by monitoring a Wikipedia list.[16]

Number of active platforms

We counted the number of active platforms on the bitcoin chart platform per week. The variable controls for the normative legitimacy reflected in the consistency of the actions within new market emergence with the prevalent norms and values (Suchman, 1995).

Regions

We also controlled for culturally influenced trading effects in different regions. Countries were clustered in regions based on the Global Leadership and Organizational Behavior Effectiveness (GLOBE)[17] study, as well as its extension (Mensah & Chen, 2013). The region "Anglo" is used as the baseline reference category.

Regulative legitimacy (Legal, Restricted, Prohibited)

The three categories are used to measure the level of regulative legitimacy in a particular country on a weekly basis. *Legal* means that the trading of bitcoins is allowed in a particular country. *Restricted* refers to restricted trading in a given country (e.g., with regard to a particular trading field such as only for private persons), while *Prohibited* signifies that bitcoin trading is forbidden. Coding was based on several websites (e.g., industry webpages,[18] the coindance platform, newspapers and various press releases).[19]

Year

We also controlled for time effects by integrating a year-based variable.

Results

Descriptive results

Table 12.1 depicts the descriptive statistics for the variables used in this study. The correlation matrix shows that most variables did not demonstrate multicollinearity ($r < 0.498$). Only the correlation between corruption and the voice and accountability variable is higher ($r = 0.736$). Therefore, we included the variables in our regressions separately with consistent results. In addition, all variance inflation factors (VIF) are below 3, far below the recommended ceiling of 10 (Neter et al., 1996).[20]

Table 12.1 Descriptive statistics and correlation table

#	Variable	VIF	Mean	Std. Dev.	Min.	Max.	1	2	3	4	5	6	7	8	9	10	11
1	DV: Bitcoin trading volume (ln)	1.63	14.255	4.808	0	30.971											
2	Corruption	2.88	0.459	1.152	−1.44	2.4	−0.143										
3	Voice and accountability	2.88	0.287	0.960	−1.88	1.74	−0.159	0.736									
4	Interest rate	1.1	4.829	7.194	−16.539	41.985	0.107	−0.232	−0.123								
5	Google bitcoin attention	1.47	11.902	17.036	0	100	0.348	−0.195	−0.138	0.054							
6	No. alternative cryptocurrencies	1.14	5.101	3.065	1	13	−0.066	−0.058	−0.034	−0.041	−0.249						
7	No. of active platforms	1.28	2.112	2.675	1	22	0.211	0.293	0.216	−0.052	−0.075	0.02					
8	Regions	1.34	6.139	3.316	1	12	0.038	−0.424	−0.413	0.133	0.095	0.063	−0.298				
9	Legal	1.63	0.499	0.500	0	1	0.095	0.374	0.312	0.033	0.051	0.016	0.182	−0.163			
10	Restricted	1.16	0.040	0.196	0	1	0.216	−0.038	−0.046	−0.053	0.069	−0.096	−0.037	0.028	−0.167		
11	Prohibited	1.45	0.064	0.246	0	1	0.172	−0.224	−0.461	0.042	0.006	0.053	0.022	0.094	−0.246	−0.047	
12	Year	2.08	2015.335	2.017	2010	2018	0.498	−0.184	−0.124	0.112	0.514	−0.213	−0.067	0.153	0.299	0.167	−0.008
	Mean VIF	1.67															

Table 12.2 Fixed-effects panel regression on weekly bitcoin trading

Variable	Model 1	Model 2	Model 3	Model 4
Corruption		−1.635***		−0.813**
		(0.296)		(0.303)
Voice and accountability			−4.337***	−4.109***
			(0.349)	(0.359)
Interest rate	0.124***	0.120***	0.132***	0.130***
	(0.009)	(0.009)	(0.009)	(0.009)
Google bitcoin attention	0.037***	0.037***	0.037***	0.037***
	(0.002)	(0.002)	(0.002)	(0.002)
No. alternative cryptocurrencies	−0.080***	−0.080***	−0.100***	−0.098***
	(0.018)	(0.018)	(0.018)	(0.018)
No. of active platforms	0.481***	0.493***	0.506***	0.510***
	(0.025)	(0.025)	(0.025)	(0.025)
Regions	dropped	dropped	dropped	dropped
Legal	1.078***	0.991***	0.868***	0.836***
	(0.120)	(0.121)	(0.121)	(0.121)
Restricted	0.586**	0.752***	0.829***	0.895***
	(0.187)	(0.190)	(0.188)	(0.189)
Prohibited	1.601***	1.688***	1.641***	1.682***
	(0.168)	(0.169)	(0.167)	(0.168)
Year	Included	Included	Included	Included
Constant	6.515***	7.026***	8.229***	8.366***
	(0.430)	(0.439)	(0.449)	(0.452)
N	11696	11476	11476	11476
R–Square	0.492	0.495	0.5	0.5
Prob > F	0.000***	0.000***	0.000***	0.000***

Legend: † $p < 0.1$; * $p < 0.05$; ** $p < 0.01$; *** $p < 0.001$

Regression results

The results of our hypotheses tests are depicted in Table 12.2.[21] In H1, we assumed that a higher level of corruption perception in a country is positively related to bitcoin trading. In contrast to H1, we find (Table 12.2, Model 4) that, surprisingly, the coefficient of restriction is negative and highly significant ($ß = 3.346$, $p < 0.01$), not supporting our H1. In H2, we assumed that a higher voice and accountability perception in a country is negatively related to bitcoin trading. We find (Table 12.2, Model 4) that the coefficient of restriction is negative and highly significant ($ß = −4.109$, $p < 0.001$), lending support to our H2.

Discussion and conclusion

The aim of this study was to investigate how corruption and market effectiveness impacted bitcoin trading from 2010 to 2018 in different geoeconomic, i.e., institutional, settings. Our first finding indicates that a higher level of corruption perception in a country is negatively related to bitcoin trading, which contrasts with the widespread belief that cryptocurrency trading is often used to circumvent capital controls, to evade taxes and to finance illegal or black-market activities. In fact, our finding supports the notion that in countries with high corruption perception, cryptocurrency trading seems to be limited. This implies that bitcoins and the underlying technology (blockchain) may have the potential to provide a decentralized, globally available and therefore efficient way to conduct international financial and other Internet-based transactions, and store data via a system that is more (instead of less) resilient toward corruption than expected. However, there is currently a lack of an appropriate legal and regulatory framework in many countries with many legal questions that require resolution not only locally but globally.

Our second finding, that a higher voice and accountability perception in a country is negatively related to bitcoin trading, supports the contention that press freedom and the availability of free and independent media serve a key role in informing market participants about underlying risks of investments (Bhattacharya et al., 2009), as well as about the rules of the game (Dyck et al., 2008), e.g., by publicly announcing new or planned regulations. The finding further supports the argument that the governance environment antecedes the chosen investment mode (Li & Filer, 2007). Regarding bitcoin trading, our findings show that cryptocurrencies might be an alternative investment and offer a way to conduct financial transactions in countries that suffer from sanctions or hyperinflation, such as Iran or Venezuela (e.g., Haseborg et al., 2019), which future research could explore.

Over time, as blockchain costs decline and scalability increases, we expect increasing cryptocurrency adoption by governments and institutions, particularly in emerging markets with simultaneous global coordination of governance. Practically, the results of our study also imply that the potential benefits of cryptocurrency trading may outweigh their societal costs and, by extension, that rapid adoption in the wider financial services sector and the rise of specialized cryptocurrency investment advisories can be expected.

Notes

1 https://thenextweb.com/hardfork/2019/12/13/satoshi-nakaboto-bitcoins-market-cap-is-now-on-par-with-costcos/ (accessed January 10, 2020).
2 Narrow stock of money is the "total quantity of currency in circulation (notes and coins) plus demand deposits denominated in the national currency, held by non-bank financial institutions, state and local governments, nonfinancial public enterprises, and the private sector of the economy" (www.cia.gov/library/publications/the-world-factbook/rankorder/2214rank.html) (accessed September 12, 2018).
3 Government-backed digital tokens are also referred to as central bank digital currencies (CDBCs).
4 Certainly, the speed of both legal and illegal transactions can be greatly accelerated with blockchain technology. Speed is often a factor in the success of a crime.
5 www.interpol.int/News-and-media/News/2018/N2018-022 (accessed October 10, 2018).

6 https://bitcoincharts.com (accessed October 29, 2019).
7 www.transparency.rog; data are available from http://files.transparency.org/content/download/2155/13635/file/CPI2016_FullDataSetWithRegionalTables.xlsx (accessed September 12, 2018).
8 www.transparency.org/research/cpi (accessed September 12, 2018).
9 The six dimensions are (1) voice and accountability, (2) political stability and absence of violence/terrorism, (3) government effectiveness, (4) regulatory quality, (5) rule of law and (6) control of corruption.
10 http://info.worldbank.org/governance/wgi/#home (accessed March 23, 2019).
11 We followed earlier studies (e.g., Roulet & Touboul, 2015) and used a linear prediction for GDP per capita (in current USD) for Venezuela, based on the last five years because later data were not available.
12 http://info.worldbank.org/governance/wgi/#home (accessed March 23, 2019).
13 https://datacatalog.worldbank.org/voice-and-accountability-percentile-rank (as accessed on October 29, 2019).
14 https://data.worldbank.org/indicator/fr.inr.rinr (accessed October 29, 2019).
15 https://trends.google.com/trends/explore?q=bitcoin (accessed September 12, 2018).
   Following prior research (e.g., Kristoufek, 2013, 2015), we obtained the search requests for the search term "bitcoin" via Google Trends. Note that these data are relative. Google Trends states: "Numbers represent search interest relative to the highest point on the chart for the given region and time. A value of 100 is the peak popularity for the term. A value of 50 means that the term is half as popular. Likewise, a score of zero means the term was less than 1% as popular as the peak." To normalize the distribution of this variable, we used the natural log.
16 https://en.wikipedia.org/wiki/List_of_cryptocurrencies (accessed on June 1, 2018).
17 https://globeproject.com/results/clusters/latin-america?menu=list#list (accessed on October 1, 2019).
18 www.bitcoinmarketjournal.com/bitcoin-regulation-by-country/ (accessed October 19, 2018).
19 www.loc.gov/law/help/cryptocurrency/cryptocurrency-world-survey.pdf (accessed October 19, 2018).
20 This is calculated as VIF = $1/(1 - R_i^2)$ where i is the relevant predictor variable.
21 The Hausman (1978) test indicated that the fixed effects (FE) estimator is more appropriate (p < 0.001). Therefore, we estimated our regressions based on the FE estimator. However, we also ran a random effects (RE) regression with consistent results.

References

Adler, P. A. (1993). *Wheeling and Dealing. An Ethnography of an Upper-Level Drug Dealing and Smuggling Community*. New York: Columbia University Press.
Akerlof, G. (1970). The market for "lemons": Quality uncertainty and the market mechanism. *The Quarterly Journal of Economics*, 84 (3), 488–500.
Andersson, H. (2003). Illegal entrepreneurs. A comparative study of the liquor trade in Stockholm and New Orleans 1920–1940. *Journal of Scandinavian Studies in Criminology and Crime Prevention*, 3, 114–134.
Becker, G. S. (1968). Crime and punishment. An economic approach. *Journal of Political Economy*, 76, 169–217.
Bhattacharya, U., Galpin, N., Ray, R., and Yu, X. (2009). The role of the media in the internet IPO bubble. *Journal of Financial and Quantitative Analysis*, 44 (3), 657–682.
Bjerg, O. (2016). How is Bitcoin money? *Theory, Culture & Society*, 33, 53–72.
Böhme, R., Christin, N., Edelman, B., and Moore, T. (2015). Bitcoin. Economics, technology, and governance. *Journal of Economic Perspectives*, 29, 213–238.

Cheah, E.-T., and Fry, J. (2015). Speculative bubbles in Bitcoin markets? An empirical investigation into the fundamental value of Bitcoin. *Economics Letters*, 130, 32–36.

Christin, N. (2013). Traveling the silk road. In D. Schwabe (ed.), *Proceedings of the 22nd International Conference on World Wide Web* (pp. 213–224). Geneva: ACM Digital Library. Republic and Canton of Geneva: International World Wide Web Conferences Steering Committee.

Cuervo-Cazurra, A. (2006). Who cares about corruption? *Journal of International Business Studies*, 37, 807–822.

Dimaggio, P. J., and Powell, W. W. (1983). The iron cage revisited: Institutional isomorphism and collective rationality in organizational fields. *American Sociological Review*, 147–160.

Dyck, A., Volchkova, N., and Zingales, L. (2008). The corporate governance role of the media: Evidence from Russia. *The Journal of Finance*, 63 (3), 1093–1135.

Estrin, S., Korosteleva, J., and Mickiewicz, T. (2013). Which institutions encourage entrepreneurial growth aspirations? *Journal of Business Venturing*, 28, 564–580.

Geroski, P. (2003). *The Evolution of New Markets*. Oxford: Oxford University Press.

Goudie, A. W., and Stasavage, D. (1998). A framework for the analysis of corruption. *Crime, Law and Social Change*, 29, 113–159.

Habib, M., and Zurawicki, L. (2002). Corruption and foreign direct investment. *Journal of International Business Studies*, 33, 291–307.

Haseborg, V. T., Macho, A., and Schlesiger, C. (2019). Operation hinterzimmer. *Wirtschaftswoche*, 23, 60–62.

Hausman, J. A. (1978). Specification tests in econometrics. *Econometrica*, 46 (6), 1251–1271.

Isaak, A., and Bort, S. (2019). *When No Means Yes: Exploring Prohibition-Legitimacy Dynamics in New Market Emergence*. Working Paper, World Bank.

Jensen, M. C., and Meckling, W. H. (1976). Theory of the firm: Managerial behavior, agency costs and ownership structure. *Journal of Financial Economics*, 3 (4), 305–360.

Kaufmann, D., Kraay, A., and Mastruzzi, M. (2010). *The Worldwide Governance Indicators. A Summary of Methodology, Data and Analytical Issues*. World Bank Policy Research Working Paper No. 5430. Retrieved August 25, 2020, from http://info.worldbank.org/gov ernance/wgi/pdf/wgi.pdf.

Kristoufek, L. (2013). Bitcoin meets Google Trends and Wikipedia. Quantifying the relationship between phenomena of the Internet era. *Scientific Reports*, 3, 3415.

Kristoufek, L. (2015). What are the main drivers of the Bitcoin price? Evidence from wavelet coherence analysis. *PloS One*, 10 (4), e0123923.

Li, S., and Filer, L. (2007). The effects of the governance environment on the choice of investment mode and the strategic implications. *Journal of World Business*, 42, 89–98.

Malkiel, B. G., and Fama, E. F. (1970). Efficient capital markets: A review of theory and empirical work. *The Journal of Finance*, 25 (2), 383–417.

Mensah, Yaw M., and Chen, Hsiao-Yin (2013). *Global Clustering of Countries by Culture – An Extension of the GLOBE Study*. April 14. Retrieved from SSRN: https://ssrn.com/abstract=2189904.

Meyer, J. W., and Rowan, B. (1977). Institutionalized organizations: Formal structure as myth and ceremony. *American Journal of Sociology*, 83 (2), 340–363.

Nakamoto, S. (2008). *Bitcoin: A Peer-to-Peer Electronic Cash System*. Retrieved from http://bitcoin. org/bitcoin.pdf.

Neter, J., Kutner, M. H., Nachtsheim, C. J., and Wasserman, W. (1996). *Applied Linear Statistical Models*. Chicago: Irwin.

North, D. C. (1990). *Institutions, Institutional Change, and Economic Performance*. Cambridge, MA: Harvard University Press.

Pigou, A. C. (1917). The value of money. *The Quarterly Journal of Economics*, 32 (1), 38–65.

Punwasi, S. (2017). *Evading Chinese Capital Controls*. Retrieved from https://betterdwelling. com/evading-chinese-capital-controls-101-bitcoin-expert-dr-joseph-wang/.

Roulet, T. J., and Touboul, S. (2015). The intentions with which the road is paved: Attitudes to liberalism as determinants of greenwashing. *Journal of Business Ethics*, 128 (2), 305–320.

Scott, W. R. (1995). *Institutions and Organizations*. 1st Edition. Thousand Oaks, CA: Sage.

Sine, W. D., Haveman, H. A., and Tolbert, P. S. (2005). Risky business? Entrepreneurship in the new independent-power sector. *Administrative Science Quarterly*, 50, 200–232.

Stephan, U., Uhlaner, L. M., and Stride, C. (2015). Institutions and social entrepreneurship. The role of institutional voids, institutional support, and institutional configurations. *Journal of International Business Studies*, 46, 308–333.

Stix, H. (2013). Why do people save in cash? Distrust, memories of banking crises, weak institutions and dollarization. *Journal of Banking and Finance*, 37 (11), 4087–4106.

Suchman, M. C. (1995). Managing legitimacy. Strategic and institutional approaches. *Academy of Management Review*, 20, 571–610.

Tanzi, V. (1995). Corruption, government activities and markets. *Finance & Development*, 32, 24.

US Supreme Court. (1987). *Carpenter vs. the United States. No. 86-422. FindLaw | Cases and Codes*. Retrieved August 20, 2012, from Caselaw.lp.findlaw.com.

Weber, B. (2014). Bitcoin and the legitimacy crisis of money. *Cambridge Journal of Economics*, 40 (1), 17–41.

Wei, S.-J. (2000). How taxing is corruption on international investors? *Review of Economics and Statistics*, 82, 1–11.

Index

Note: Page numbers in *italics* indicate a figure and page numbers in **bold** indicate a table on the corresponding page.